My unseen friends and artists,

I go from this place reluct[antly, a]
little sadder for the separation, y[et] happier
[fo]r my earning. In these past three weeks
[I] have lived my fantasy: to sojourn on a
[re]mote island wilderness with a couple of
[goo]d books (including "The Good Book"), my
[pa]ints and the love of my life, Marlene.

It will not take you long to bond with
[thi]s charming cottage. Her personality will
[be] revealed in every cupboard and drawer
[an]d in each slightly askew wall and shelf
[The] water pump wishes to exercise its
[in]dependence. However, with a few kind
[w]ords spoken in encouragement, it will
[br]ing forth a generous stream of water. My
[m]ethod was to remove the pump cap (the
[pi]pe wrench is in the front porch tool
[ca]binet) which is closest to the pump
[ha]ndle and prime the pump with water

I came to heal and Isle Royale helped. To just be, is a great gift and this island allowed that. I found the sounds of nature and the sights of the island very awe striking and inspiring. I thank the Park Service & staff for hosting me & I hope that the painting I give them will convey the beauty I feel. I thank my son Dan for coming for a week and portaging the canoe for me so I could see as much of the island as possible. I've never caught a northern pike before and catching a 2's footer was one of my highlights. As far as we could tell we were the only people on Intermediate Lake. The scenery is incredibly

THE ISLAND

ISLE ROYALE ARTISTS IN RESIDENCE 1991–1998

WITHIN US

EDITED AND COMPILED BY
Robert Root
Jill Burkland

Isle Royale Natural History Association
Houghton, Michigan

ISBN: 0-935289-12-7 Cloth
0-935289-11-9 Paper

Library of Congress Catalog Card Number: 99-085909

Book Designed by Christina Watkins
Project Management by Jill Burkland
Typography and Production by Penny Smith, TypeWorks
Printing by Imperial Litho & Dryography, Phoenix, Arizona

michigan council for
arts and cultural affairs

This project was made possible with the support of the Michigan
Council for the Arts and Cultural Affairs.

This publication is printed on quality coated paper manufactured on acid
free base to insure its long life. Publication was made possible, in part, by
the generous support of the Mead Paper Division.

Cover Art, segment of Isle Royale Portage
   by Elizabeth Holster, 1996
Frontispiece, Moose Studies
   by Gerald Korte, 1995

Contents

The Island Within Us: Artists on Isle Royale

Robert Root

When I first saw *Isle Royale Reflections*, the program about artists-in-residence on Isle Royale, I was entranced with the image of poet Keith Taylor writing by lantern light in front of a long row of windows looking out on Tobin Harbor. The camera, outside the cabin, slowly drew back to a long view of the cabin, the water, the woods, the glow of sunset. I thought, "If this is what being an artist in residence is like, I have to become one."

Artists seek residencies for time and distance—time to be immersed in their art, distance from a world of distractions. They hope to go someplace that renews their spirit, their vision, their dedication to their art.

But a residency in Isle Royale National Park, so remote and undeveloped, adds another level to the meaning of time and distance. This isn't a retreat, a sojourn in a comfortable hideaway; it's a withdrawal, a total immersion in a different way of living. The artist takes a residency in an earlier century.

The Dassler cabin, where the artists now stay, perches on a short, flat bluff across a small shallow cove from the tip of Scoville Point. A weathered wooden bench on the north end of the bluff looks out on Tobin Harbor and the channel toward Passage Island. Trees surrounding the cabin give little shelter from lake winds. Sunrise through living room windows is spectacular when you see it across all that open water. Sunset behind interior island ridges is simply a gleaming golden band of brightness reflecting off the water.

It's a small cabin. The unheated bedroom stays dark in the morning; the kitchen is narrow and cramped; the large pine paneled main room has two birch tree trunks running across the length of the ceiling, a birch tree bench and table at the east end, and a stone fireplace with heat ducts above and at the sides to circulate heat (ineffectively). The cabin is cozy when it's warm and can almost overheat on sunny days.

Dassler Cabin
oil on canvas
18″ × 24″
Gijsbert van Frankenhuyzen, 1992

Cabin dwellers need to work for common necessities—pump and filter water from the lake, gather and chop firewood, fill lanterns and replace wicks, exist for two or three weeks on supplies they themselves have brought from the mainland. In the cabin's log departing artists often leave advice and record impressions about rustic living. One artist was glad for the company of someone who recognized "the more arcane, historical and useful items (like the stovetop heat spreader that lets you keep coffee warm or toast an English muffin)." Someone else advised about firewood: "Beaver-chewed birch is much nicer than downfall birch—it is seasoned and burns like coal. For kindling—consult the dead balsam beside the guest house. Branches covered w/ usnea [beardmoss] go up like a rocket. Birch bark is a sure-fire starter." Not all the practical advice is about cabin chores: "Be careful if you skinny dip at dawn. sometimes hikers actually appear on the ridge at that early hour."

Daily living becomes a vital aspect of the residency, weaning artists away from off-island worries and freeing them to concentrate on experiencing the island. A writer noted in the cabin's log, "I've spent two weeks learning not to care if the pump entirely fills the cistern; repairing the pump; moving around in the dark without flashlight or lantern; studying the mosses & liverworts of Scoville Point; fish watching; anticipating—& then seeing—the northern lights." A painter wrote: "The solitude, the intensity of landscape, the lack of interruptions to devote to my landscape painting has been incredible. I am enjoying the necessities: cutting wood, getting water, building fires to keep warm. . . . Does life get better than this? I think not."

The artists are based in the Dassler cabin but they often range widely over the island. Like other visitors they take in tours, travel to other parts of the island, hike the trails, and canoe Tobin and Rock Harbors. Adjusting to cabin life takes up early days but soon learning to see the island becomes primary. As a musician writes in her artist statement, the residency "gave me a chance to look into myself (including meeting some fears), acclimate to the rhythms and moods of the lake and island, and feel a joining of art and place." A poet described it as a "pleasing return to an integrated life," one that didn't make him "compartmentalize the various activities I live by." For him the island offered "not a respite or a retreat but a full charge directly into a subject. . . . I found that whatever I was doing—observing a moose feeding, chopping the day's firewood, or doing dishes by candlelight, I was gathering material."

Seeing—simply seeing—becomes an important activity in the residency. In the cabin log a painter wrote that she "found the hardest challenge was deciding how to balance the art-making & the rambling & the just-sitting-and-being. I think I made the right choices . . . just sitting and listening was truly fine." A photographer addressed the balance between art and place well (and also provided a handy catalog of sights) when he wrote: "I found the work a challenge—the play a delight. . . . This residency has provided the isolation from the demands of my 'normal' existence to fully participate in pondering. Sun, moon, stars, wind, rain, blazing blue sky. Sunrise, sunset, mergansers, hawks, ducks, teal, cormorants, gulls and tweety birds. Loons, moose, foxes, squirrels, toads, three different woodpeckers and more scat than you can count. . . . And lest we forget, wolf howls, rainbows, and an amazing aurora borealis. "

The artists often have to learn how to work on the island, how to deal with its challenging, changeable environment. Expecting to work several days in a row on a landscape painting she had just begun, an artist arrived at her location the next day to find "the weather was entirely different. So was the lighting and the shadows and, seemingly, everything else." Needless to say, this altered the way she worked. Many visual artists relied on extensive sketchbooks to create materials that would lead to finished work off-island; the verbal artists took with them journal entries, notes, and rough drafts. Much begun outdoors in sunlight was completed indoors by lanternlight.

This deep immersion Isle Royale residency affects not only the artists' work but also the artists themselves. Their comments register the impact of their time on the island:

- A photographer: *"This residency has been the most intensive photography I have ever done."*

- A musician: *"Clarity, strength, complexity, and delicate beauty; these are all qualities of Isle Royale. It has become a part of me, my music, my spirit."*

- A painter: *"I relearned how to see while I worked in my sketchbook . . . it gave me special pleasure that my paintings were created using Lake Superior on my brush."*

- A painter: *"My memories of Isle Royale, my breakthroughs of observation and of fear, continue to strengthen my determination and my work."*

- A photographer: *"I have a quieter, less dramatic approach to the landscape and photography now."*

- A painter: *"The in-depth experience afforded by the Artist-in-Residence Program has made the drawings I have done of the island setting stronger, richer, and deeper."*

At the end of my own residency, taking the Ranger back to the mainland, I thought the return passage should be a strictly observed period of mourning. But even then I knew what my writing had gained from the island and I am still drawing upon journal entries from my island days.

The residency has a long-lasting effect. The artistic results of the Isle Royale Artist-in-Residence Program are evident in this book. But the artists themselves feel enriched by the experience. One photographer wrote, ". . . we were blessed. This place gave us as much as we could take & gave us more than we expected." A painter called it "a brief two week love affair, a romance of blinding passion, with this place, this rock and land, and sunlight. Being here has been like painting naked, leaving all the barriers behind, allowing all the elements to touch and mark us, to mark me." A musician described feeling "like I've been 'drinking in' this place . . . storing it in the cells of my body for the upcoming year."

In his log entry at the cabin Gary Lawless copied one of his poems which ended:

> *We walk the ridge lines*
> *thirsting for everything:*
> *That yellow flower,*
> *That bird overhead.*
> *Without knowing, we drink,*
> *and leave with the island*
> *inside of us.*

That image captures the feelings of Isle Royale's artists about what they take away from the island.

It's difficult to leave without having taken the island within us. For Isle Royale's artists-in-residence, however, the island within us re-emerges in the art it inspires. That, in the end, is what we hope this book commemorates.

So Many Other Spirits Are There: The Dassler Cabin

Scattered at the east and west ends of Isle Royale are cabins reminiscent of an earlier age—cabins built almost a century ago as resort homes for families from around the midwest. When Isle Royale became a National Park in 1940 these cabins were either purchased by the National Park Service or were retained by families with life leases to expire at the death of their named beneficiary. Two of these historic cottages have been home to Isle Royale's artists in residence.

Interior of the Dassler Cottage

For the first two years of the Isle Royale Artists in Residence Program, artists were housed in the Kemmer cabin across Tobin Harbor on Hidden Lake. Elizabeth Kemmer, who previously owned the cabin, was a long-time summer resident and an artist. A charming cabin with a beautiful view, the Kemmer Cabin was perhaps too isolated. As Keith Taylor remembers, "The only ways back to Rock Harbor were either a vigorous canoe down and across the inlet, or a hike of several hours duration up to Lookout Louise, then along the Greenstone Trail until I could cut south at the bottom of Tobin Harbor. It was easier to stay alone as much as possible."

When the Dassler cabin in Tobin Harbor fell to the park in 1992 it was decided that its easy access to Rock Harbor made it a more suitable home for our island artists and it has been home to Isle Royale's artists-in-residence ever since. For the artists who have lived there the Dassler cabin has been a quiet haven, a source of warmth and light, a shelter from cold and storms. In his diary Richard Schilling describes how his bonding with the cottage began his first evening there: "I found the cottage that would be my home for the next three weeks sequestered under pines and birch on a rocky promontory thirty feet above the waters of Tobin Harbor. Inside, the cottage walls and furniture are slightly askew to a plum line, yet they welcome me as a similarly flawed friend. The wavy windowpanes sparkle with jewel-like air inclusions. A skilled stone mason built the fireplace and hewed from a log its decorative mantle. Even though it is now late in the evening, the light is only beginning to fade. It has not been necessary to burn the kerosene lamps."

The views from the bench in front of the cabin have been an inspiration not only for painters but for writers and musicians as well.

Composer Sheila Larkin described it this way, "From that bench I saw the northern lights and amazing sunsets and heard the rush of gulls and loons above and mergansers below. At the height of that point you share the sky with the birds and can be startled awake in early morning hours by the call of a loon as it wings just over the roof of the cabin. I spent many hours at that bench reading, singing, and taking in the sights and spirit of the place. It is an honored spot."

Lee Dassler, a descendent of Isle Royale's Dassler family as well as an artist-in-residence, had the chance to revisit her old family cabin and left this entry in the logbook:

Left: Dassler Family, ca. 1906

Right: Original Dassler Dock

June 16, 1996

> *Born and raised in Missouri myself, I have never questioned my great grandparents' desire to purchase this land from a copper company in the late 1880s. Charles Frederick William Dassler was a graduate of St. Louis University Law School in the 1860s and served as a justice on the first Supreme Court of Kansas. His wife Lee was an artist and arts promoter. They lived in Leavenworth, Kansas, over-looking the Missouri River. (If you've ever been to Kansas in August you'd know why tenting here in the summer was preferable!)*
>
> *Their son, John Carl Dassler, summered here all of his life. He helped build the main cabin (built to over-winter boats initially—and later to shelter family) as well as the sleeping cabin. JC designed and built the fireplace in 1947. JC met Lucy Finlayson of Omaha in Tobin Harbor—she was visiting the island with her friend Gertrude How (How Island is small and has two cabins on it, one red).*
>
> *In '36 Lucy and JC commissioned a boat from builders in Portage Entry, the Awinita, which was kept at the Anderson boat dock when they were in Tobin. From that point on, Isle Royale was*

their base for long voyages around the Great Lakes with their children, Margaret and Dale, and their spaniel Corky. Margaret married Bill Lichte and they had one child, Richard, who is now a theater director in New York City.

Dale married "Ibbie" Franke and had three kids—Skip, Steve and me.

Of that whole cast of characters, Richard Lichte, Skip Dassler, and myself are the only ones left. So this cabin is very rich in spirit. Not only does she provide beautiful views and protection from storms and wind, but she harbors our family memory. These two little cabins are the only common ground shared by four generations of Dasslers.

I am so thankful that the NPS and IRNHA allowed me to return here for these June days. It has been a real centering for me— and wonderful to try to document the beauty of the remaining cottages and buildings in Tobins. So many other spirits are here.

Enjoy the cabin. Take care of her.

The spirits of the Dassler family and their island friends continue to inhabit the Dassler cabin on Isle Royale's Tobin Harbor. They have been joined now by the spirits of Isle Royale's artists-in-residence— painters, writers, musicians and sculptors who have left something of themselves behind at this special site. So many spirits are here, and more will join them as the Dassler Cabin continues to house Isle Royale's artists-in-residence into our new century.

A Whispering Park:
The Artist-in-Residence

A whisper or a shout—which is harder to hear? Which is seasoned in mystery and shrouded in mystique? Which sets the stage for self-discovery, is more intimate, and lends itself to many interpretations? Isle Royale National Park is a whispering resource with few, if any scenic shouts. Many parks shout through the eruption of Old Faithful, the expanse of the Grand Canyon, or the grand sculpture of Mount Rushmore. For casual visitors these shouts fulfill their curiosity in a matter of minutes. Once fulfilled, they venture to the next park or scenic turnout. A whispering park's experience is quite different. Isle Royale's average visitors will immerse themselves for four or five days in a landscape filled with self-discovery. The intimacy of the park and its many interpretations set the cornerstone that Isle Royale National Park's Artist-in-Residence Program is built upon.

The initial planning stage for the Artist-in-Residence Program was set in the fall of 1990. The park's goal was to establish a long term program that would be supported through the expertise of several partners. Partnerships were developed with the Isle Royale Natural History Association and the Copper Country Community Arts Council—partnerships that continue today.

The concept for the program was fairly straightforward. In exchange for passage on the *Ranger III*, a place to stay, use of a canoe and some help with groceries, the park asked artists to experience the island and capture the magic they found through the medium they pursued. They were expected to do two or three programs for park visitors and to donate a representative piece of their work to the park's permanent collection. That collection is displayed in park visitor centers and has been and will continue to be exhibited in galleries around the region.

In the winter of 1991, a jury of four was selected, consisting of two members from the Copper Country Community Arts Council and a member each from the National Park and the Isle Royale Natural History Association. The jury developed the selection criteria, length of stay, and several other procedures that are still used today. The first year of the program, thirty-three applications were received and three artists were selected, sculptor Julia Barello, poet Keith Taylor, and photographer Jeff Korte.

The site for the 1991 program was the Kemmer cabin near Hidden Lake in secluded Tobin Harbor. After the death of its owner, Elizabeth Kemmer, who held a life lease on the cabin, the park took ownership and interested individuals and Copper Country businesses provided furnishings.

The second year of the program was an ambitious one. Eighty applications were received and seven artists were selected. A second cabin was added to house artists, the Dassler family residence at the end of Scoville Point in Tobin Harbor. The logistics involved in using two cabins proved to be too much for the Park Service to administer, so from 1993 on all artists have been housed in the Dassler cabin. In 1995 volunteers Greg McHuron (1994 Artist-in-Residence), Eric McHuron, and Frank Azzolino repaired the roof, floors and foundation, securing the cabin for many more years of service to Isle Royale artists-in-residence.

Over the years, the program has taken on its own identity, providing countless benefits to Isle Royale National Park, its visitors, the Tobin Harbor community and local residents of the Copper Country. Lifelong friendships have been developed, human souls have been recharged, spirits have been renewed, and lives have been re-examined and changed. The artists have inspired a strong appreciation for the arts and provided different perspectives, allowing others to see the park in a new light. *The Island Within Us* is an example of how the program will go beyond the boundaries of Isle Royale National park to share artists' interpretations of a magical whispering resource to a new audience, one that may never get a chance to visit this special place.

Isle Royale National Park has assisted several state and national parks with the development of their own artist-in-residence programs. Since 1991, twenty-six national parks have developed artist programs and the number continues to climb. The parks that shout through the eruption of Old Faithful or through sights like El Capitan and Half Dome have resident artist programs. These programs will allow the visitor to go beyond the shouts and find the creative whispers that open the door to self-discovery and provide countless benefits to the park, its visitors, and the local community.

A whisper or a shout, which is harder to hear? Which is seasoned in mystery and shrouded in mystique? Which sets the stage for self-discovery, is more intimate, and lends itself to many interpretations? Artistically, a shout lends itself to very little interpretation. A whisper, on the other hand, is artistically alive and can be interpreted from many different perspectives, which is evident in *The Island Within Us.*

Here are just a few of the wildflowers that are indigenous to Isle Royale. I found these growing next to the cottage wood pile. Wood lilies, yarro, eastern paint brush, clover, ox eye daisies and buttercups blossom in this splendid woodland mosaic. Elsewhere, the woods are gloriously carpeted with Canada dogwood, thimble berries, asters, lilies-of-the-valley, and wild iris.

The commercial fishermen of Lake Superior used these giant reels to dry out their nets and to reveal areas in need of repair.

Lake trout were suspended from rods and smoked in barrels to flavor and preserve their food value.

17

Isle Royale sketchbook

watercolor

12″ × 18″

Richard Schilling, 1996

1991

ISLE ROYALE ARTISTS IN RESIDENCE 1991-1998

Jeff Korte

My notions about photography were being stretched by my rediscovery of pinhole photography. I suspect that my travels have always been arranged to satisfy my need to photograph. What I know for certain is that the two have always been inseparable. A camera of some sort, whether looped on my belt or fixed to a tripod, is as essential as my pocket knife, or canteen.

I measure my time on Isle Royale not in days, but in experiences. Notes written during my stay help recall the echo of geese in Tobin Harbor, the quiet presence of the moose woods, and the boom of crashing waves on Blake Point.

Here are notes from journal entries on some of the photographs I took:

Aladdin. *The Kemmer cabin sits on a finger of rock along the west shore of Tobin Harbor. The panoramic view to the east looks through windows that run from end to end. There are no curtains and the gathering light swells in the room, pushing the chill from the air. If you happen to miss the expanding sunrise, the rays eventually warm your cheek with a rosy flush of daylight.*

Boathouse. *I sat by the boathouse tonight while there was still some blue left in the sky. The in-between time when trees become silhouettes and the water is a steely blue-black. I thought I heard the beaver working near the Savage boathouse on the small island a short jump from the cabin. Sneaking a view of the harbor, I saw three moose swimming away from the island. Dripping four-legged shadows rose from the lake and stood on the thin shoal forty yards away. Mother moose checked each calf before they slipped back into the water and continued their swim to the distant band of trees across the water.*

John Snell, Tobin Harbor. *I returned to the cabin at four with plans to photograph John in his old double-ended rowboat. A beautiful boat of green and white with tandem locks for the sleek copper-tipped oars. I set up in the back with camera and tripod while John rowed up and down the harbor. The boat remained sharp while John's arms and oars and water and shore blurred during the long exposure.*

Aladdin
photograph
10″ × 8″

Boathouse

photograph

8″ × 10″

John Snell, Tobin Harbor

photograph

8″ × 10″

Julia Barello

My days at Isle Royale were filled with reading, sketching, traversing the land and water, looking, collecting, and thinking. All that was pivotal in the clarification and refinement of my key ideas as an artist because it required forced contemplation. The site itself raised the very issues at the core of my work. I have always circled around the notion of polarities—nature/culture; man/woman; intellect/body. When I was at the park, I became involved in the discussion of how to fulfill the park's mission of remaining as natural as possible. Just what could that natural state be? Did it include wolves? moose? cabins that had hosted families for generations? kayaks? fishing and timber interests? copper mining? pleasure seekers? Both the nature and the culture of Isle Royale raise these questions, not offering simple answers. Once this complexity was clear, I realized that these polarities that we structure life and thought around are merely markers which don't indicate the edges of a discussion, but instead reside like the spots in water where two stones land in proximity. Their edges overlap, distort, impact, and implicate each other. It was this idea that led to the painted and collected art piece that I made for the park.

The art that I have made since leaving Isle Royale is always about examining overlaps and intersections in life—the intersection of jewelry and medicine; the acts of observation and experience; the conflict of deifying the natural world and trapping it at the same time. I left Isle Royale with many questions, and I think back to it often as a place which crystallized issues that range from the deeply personal and artistic to the political and social. It amazes me still that a place in "nature" contains so well these discussions, arguments, and questions.

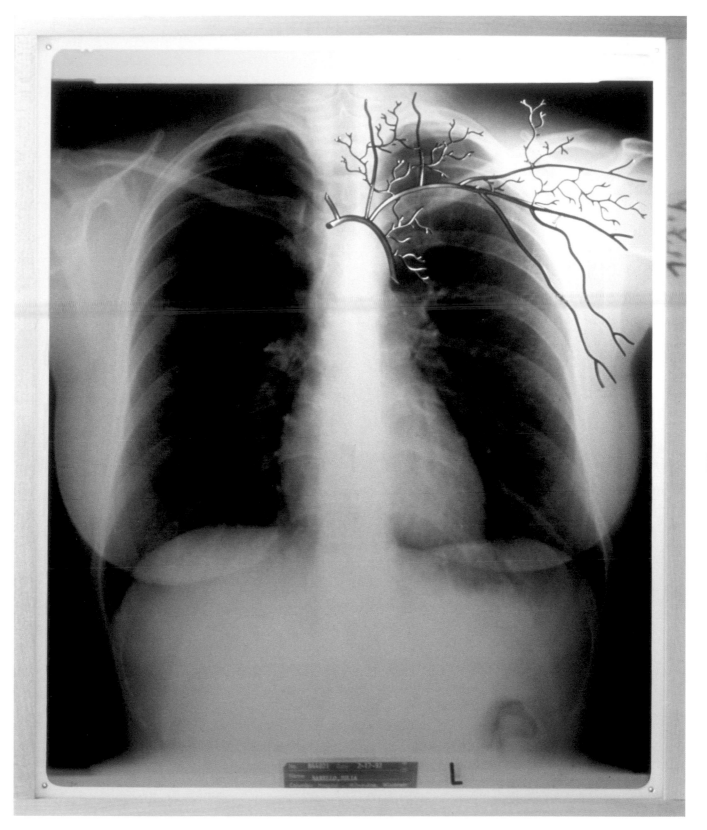

Vascular Studies III: Internal Jugular

brooch

sterling silver, x-ray, maple

1996

Keith Taylor

ABOUT THE ARTIST

Keith Taylor was born in British Columbia in 1952. He spent his childhood in Alberta and his adolescence in Indiana. After several years of traveling, he moved to Michigan, where he earned his M.A. in English at Central Michigan University. Currently, he teaches in the English Department of the University of Michigan. He lives in Ann Arbor with his wife and daughter.

His poems, stories, book reviews, personal narratives, and feature articles have appeared in well over 100 magazines, journals, anthologies, and newspapers. He has received an NEA fellowship, an ArtServe Michigan/ MCACA grant, and a Writer-in-the-Community-Residency at the Detroit YMCA, sponsored by The Writer's Voice. He has published one collection of short stories and five chapbooks of poetry, including Dream of the Black Wolf: Notes from Isle Royale.

The summer I was on Isle Royale (1991), the Artists-in-Residence were housed in the Elizabeth Kemmer cabin on the northwest side of Tobin Harbor. The only ways back to Rock Harbor were either a vigorous canoe down and across the inlet or a hike of several hours duration up to Lookout Louise, then along the Greenstone Trail until I could cut south at the bottom of Tobin Harbor. It was easier to stay alone as much as possible.

I had no specific plan for my time on the island, but even on my trip up from Ann Arbor I began compulsively entering notes in my journal. Although I've kept a journal fairly regularly for twenty-five years, during my stay on Isle Royale I wrote in it constantly: while I was cooking; when I was hiking or canoeing; when I awoke in the morning and before I went to sleep at night. Never before and only a couple of times since have I tried to record my random perceptions and emotions in such minute detail over an extended period of time. Because I was alone so much of the time, most of the references in that journal reach outside myself and bring in the extraordinary natural environment that was around me.

Over the next few months I pulled out pieces from that journal and either polished them or found ones that turned into poems when I counted syllables or heard rhythmic patterns in the words. I collected those more finished extracts in a little chapbook, *Dream of the Black Wolf: Notes from Isle Royale.* I was happy with the mix of poetry and prose. It's a form I want to try again.

I hope that the pieces in that chapbook carry some sense of that intense involvement with the process of perception as I experienced it on Isle Royale. While there I had the extraordinary opportunity of watching myself learn to see a new landscape. And that unique landscape of lake and rock, ridgeline and cedar swamp, all surrounded by the greatest body of fresh water on the planet, remains etched in my imagination with a clarity greater than almost any other landscape I have visited.

I'm here, looking out *the front window of the cabin they've provided for me. Tobin Harbor. Isle Royale. Lake Superior. The only sound other than birdcall and the occasional outboard is the high ringing of my own blood in my ears. A family of mergansers has been playing in the calm water of the passage between this window and the little island 50 or 60 yards off-shore. A loon floats through but doesn't sing. A black duck dabbles past, its bill almost phosphorescent, greenish yellow. Two spotted sandpipers fly by. Chipping sparrows are nesting in the spruce not 15 feet from the front door of this place. A late wild iris has bloomed in the four hours since I arrived. Two hours ago it was still wrapped around itself.*

THE GUEST CABIN
for EK

Blue burns in a blue world.
Wild iris—the blue flag—
uncurled in a basalt crack
below spruce and beard moss.
A greeting, if we want it,
from the woman, long dead,
who built her place where
the wail and tremolo
of loon song collect
like the vespers chants
of monks moving to prayer.
The sun at evening prisms
through their windows dappling
the altar red and blue.

I CANOED DOWN TOBIN HARBOR, *passed through Merritt Lane,*
and went out as far as I dared into the big lake. I didn't go very far,
maybe a couple of hundred yards. Superior was quiet, but the water
had a different quality than the water in the inlet or on the rivers I've
canoed. There was power underneath toying with the canoe as it
floated over the swales. I turned back to the island and beached the
canoe on the rocks below Blake Point.

I climbed out to the Point, sat and rested looking toward Passage
Island, three miles off. A few days ago a fisherman told me that he had
seen a white pelican out there.

* * *

So I imagine sitting here, warm in the sun and tired after
paddling, and seeing a white pelican flying straight in, a white giant
with pure black wing tips. But it won't happen today. It won't happen
at any moment I expect it.

DREAM OF THE BLACK WOLF

A quick glimpse

                    in my eye's
                    corner

black wolf
        running
                            always running
        ears back
        fur
                    shaggy
                    hackles up
                    a touch
                                        of white
                                        or silver
                                                    on its belly

beside the lake
over rock
and lost
                between spruce
                and cedar

                before
I turn

(Excerpts from *Dream of the Black Wolf: Notes from Isle Royale* by Keith Taylor
[Ridgeway Press, 1993]. Copyright 1993 by Keith Taylor, who has full rights to
grant reprint permissions.)

1992

Eddie Soloway

ABOUT THE ARTIST

Eddie Soloway lives in Santa Fe, New Mexico. "Since childhood my passion has been the natural world." Early days in Scouting led to a commitment to study ecology at the University of Wisconsin. After college he started a decade-long position with the Institute for Earth Education. He led teacher education workshops and developed programs designed to help people of all ages maintain a lifelong relationship with the natural world.

After a ten-year absence he returned to an early interest in photography. Today he divides his time between making fine-art photographs, teaching photographic workshops, and continuing work on a series of photographic books.

The Isle Royale experience goes beyond creating new work; it goes into that sacred realm of nurturing the soul and building the foundation of how we as artists create.

One particularly calm evening, I took the canoe out onto the lake. I felt as though I were balancing on the belly of a very large, sleeping beast. With each breath, a quiet, yet deceivingly tremendous force pushed me higher, then moments later set me down. Gentle but massive. For five days northeasterlies had prevented me from taking the canoe out beyond the harbor and into the open waters of Lake Superior. But tonight, with a full moon rising, the normally wild and awesome lake lay silent. A dark, deep blue, in the hour before pure black, the sky mirrored the lake, both melting into an edge hard to discern.

I pushed off into the cool night air, cutting a clean slice with the bow. As I left the protective waters of the harbor, a wild animal-like alertness tingled across every nerve in me. This lake, one tenth of all the fresh water in the world, was not to be messed with. The wrecks of numerous ships, big ships, lay well-preserved deep below the surface I slid across. I paddled further out—the same unexplained force that dares a child to touch his tongue against metal on an icy January morning—dipped the paddle into the rich cobalt water. Then again. And again. For many minutes I pushed further into the deepening night. Good sense took charge and I stopped paddling and looked back. I could see the shore, but not well. Then the beast took a deep breath. In the stillness my little canoe rose many feet, then just as quickly was set back down. Another breath, and back down again. This time I noticed that as I rode into a deep trough I completely lost sight of my faint view of land. Very much alive, and humbled, I carefully turned the little craft at a right angle to the next trough coming my way, and paddled towards the island.

Back in the arms of the cove I turned around and looked back at the calm. The lake took another breath and helped push me the last few feet to shore.

Iris

photograph

35mm

Lake Superior sunrise

photograph

35mm

Full moon canoe

photograph

35mm

Wayne R. Rice

ABOUT THE ARTIST

Wayne Rice was born in Chicago, Illinois. As part of a military family, he grew up in New Jersey, Louisiana, Massachusetts, and Illinois. Trained in painting, drawing, printmaking, and mixed-media, he has also worked in experimental film, computer animation, commercial art, and publications design.

He completed his university degree at the University of New Mexico at Albuquerque and received teacher certification from the University of Colorado at Boulder. He was selected as an artist-in-residence with New Mexico, Wyoming, and Isle Royale, and is currently active with the artist-in-residence program in Colorado. His drawings, prints, paintings and mixed-media works have been exhibited in juried and invitational shows across the United States and are held in many private and corporate collections.

My artistic ideas come from a variety of interests. In the recent past my work included influences from computer generated digital imagery, dream imagery, Eastern mystic religious traditions, children's art, historic Japanese *Ukiyo-e* color woodblock prints, southwestern Native American textile design, and American popular culture.

I always want my work to reflect a sense of emotional movement and a sense of the mysterious. As an artist-in-residence at Isle Royale National Park in September 1992, I wandered the forests alone with my camera for hours photographing beds of small green clover-like plants, lichens, wildflowers, piles of leaves, ferns, and tree bark. I felt like I was in a mystical land, timeless and lush with the exotic and new, so different from the dry and dusty American Southwest. I began to incorporate these "textures" into my drawings. I used a drawing technique that employs interplays of light and color, texture and pattern to define a kind of visual habitat for both representational and abstract imagery. The Isle Royale forest floor images began to appear as background patterns and "fabrics" in my artworks and continue to do so.

The Dassler cabin on Scoville Point was a special spot, wild, windblown and beautiful. The cabin was built by hand in the 1930s and the bottom half, made of natural stone, was covered in thick green moss and lichens. Small bent trees protected it from the wind. The next door tiny "bunkhouse" was my temporary studio for the next two weeks. We had no electricity, water was from a cistern, and an outhouse completed the accommodations. Most of our luggage was canned goods, diapers, and art supplies. The cabin interior was simple, comfortable, and stocked with many useful hardware items.

I spent my days roaming the nearby forest, walking the rocks along Scoville Point, changing diapers, cooking meals, and drawing in the bunkhouse. My son played on the little pebble beaches and chased island insects. With the help of a borrowed power boat we visited the far reaches of Tobin Harbor and saw fish, butterflies, moose, and many varieties of plants and birds. My time spent at Isle Royale National Park was precious to me. The island is a jewel that must be preserved and protected as wilderness.

Wood Lily

color pencil & mixed media

15" × 21"

Ladislav Hanka

ABOUT THE ARTIST

Ladislav Hanka came to etching as a biology student enrolling in occasional art classes where his first etching plate "awakened him to his vocation." He says, "I realized that drawing, philosophy, ecology and systematics were all preparation for my future as practitioner of the black arts—a life spent up to my elbows in inks, acids, copper, and rare hand-made papers." His subsequent education took him to Colorado (for a Master of Science degree in zoology), to Michigan (for an M.F.A. in printmaking), to Vienna (to study at the Academy of Applied Arts), and to Prague (to apprentice to an engraver of stamps and currency, "honing skills more useful to a counterfeiter than an artist").

I came to Isle Royale as a pilgrim. Having spent years drawing rocks, fish, cedar roots and birches throughout Michigan I finally felt prepared and worthy to approach the crown jewels in Lake Superior—a wholly unrealistic expectation to place on the political construct of a national park. I arrived with my wife Jana (also a painter) to face profound disillusionment—at the charter fishing speedboats, marina, diesel generators, sea-planes and the general invasion of internal combustion motors and noisemakers that marks America's use of nature. We had to drop our expectations and open up to the reality of Isle Royale today. The experience became something other than I expected, but much deepened by the historic and human elements. Most significantly a single three week session was enriched by the most cherished element of time, resulting in much greater and insightful productivity—the ultimate point of the residency.

The native fish became an important aspect of my work here largely due to the generosity of life-lessees and the Mattsons at Edison Fisheries, who left a lot of interesting creatures on the dock for me—both to draw and to eat. Within the Great Lakes, Isle Royale is among the last bastions of rare and endangered native fish. The variety of life histories, form and coloration is fascinating—just within the races of lake trout inhabiting the reefs nearby. Butterfly trout from the remote reefs with their winglike pectoral fins are unlike any others I've seen.

For me the dominant feeling of Isle Royale and consequently of the artwork I produced there is of geology stripped bare—life being but the thinnest of membranes stretched precariously taut, clinging to nearly barren rock. Cedars and spruce at the water's edge are memorably sculpted individuals, formed by the adversity of the border to which they cling. The beauty of this pristine landscape is bound inextricably to the harshness which natural conditions and short growing seasons have imparted to it. The sculpted, deeply acid-bitten form of the etching plates directly echoes the physical erosion of the bedrock. It is the ceaseless work of the wind, waves, and ice that have given form to this archipelago and it is this meeting place of the elements at the waterline which forms the dominant visual attribute of this landscape. Everything relates to the horizon.

Resurgent Lake Herring
drawing over etching & monoprint
14″ × 18″

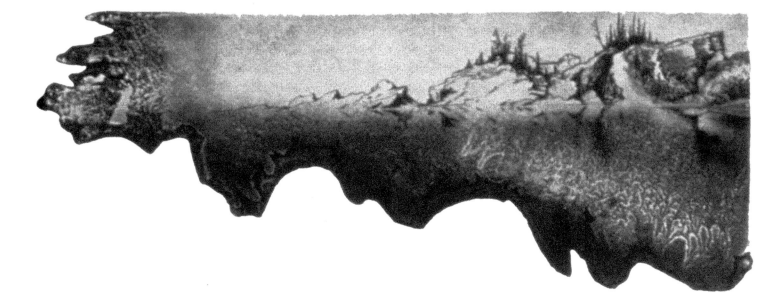

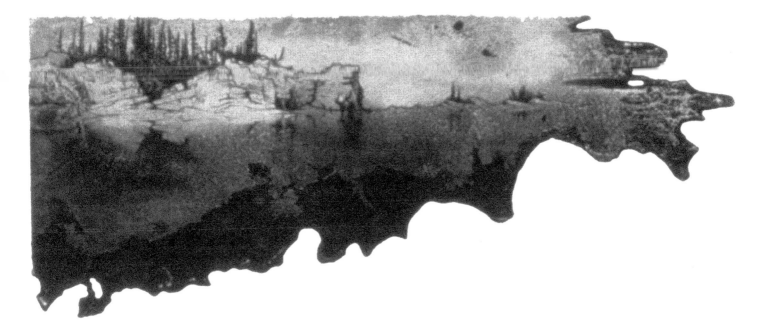

From the Depths of Minong

etching with drypoint and aquatint

8¹/₂″ × 40″

Dan Urbanski

40

I came to Isle Royale with an attitude. I felt it couldn't measure up to my Porcupine Mountains. After all, the island had no virgin timber like the Porkies, and the hills were smaller, too. But on Tobin Harbor and Scoville Point, where my wife Patty and I stayed, Lake Superior makes a profound impression. The Lake Superior impression was enhanced further because sea kayaks were our daily means of transportation. Serious regard to the lake's moods governed our comings and goings. The splendid Lake Superior scenery even crept into my subconscious: I had dreams for many weeks after the trip of the tiny islands in the harbor and waves on the rocky point.

I took home two insights from my stay on the island; one defining the mechanics of how I work, the other teaching me to look more closely at the subtleties of nature. I spent most of my sixteen-day visit just familiarizing myself with the neighborhood, finding the most scenic locations and getting some sense of the processes of nature there. Once that was accomplished, I finally got busy making meaningful images. I hadn't realized until then how critical familiarity was in creating my photographs.

My residency extended into mid-September. Near the end of my trip, I realized the Island was at the peak of autumn colors by looking down at the ground cover instead of across at the trees. The boreal forest at the east end of the island is nearly unchanging, but the wild sarsaparilla and strawberry were a riot of color. That revelation sharpened my visual acuity and has opened new photographic opportunities for me.

The photograph of the aurora borealis over Tobin Harbor was made on the first evening of my trip. After an all-day rain, the skies cleared to reveal this spectacular heavenly display. It was a special reward for a late evening trip to the outhouse.

Northern Lights

photograph

20″ × 24″

Gijsbert van Frankenhuyzen

ABOUT THE ARTIST

Born in the Netherlands, Gijsbert van Frankenhuyzen studied graphic design at the Royal Academy of Arts in Arnhem, and immigrated to the United States in 1976. In 1993, after 17 years as the Art Director for **Michigan Natural Resources Magazine,** *he ventured out on his own as an artist working on murals throughout Michigan, including exhibits at Fort Mackinac and Fort Michilimackinac. He has been widely published as an illustrator and his work can be found in* **Owls of North America, The Best of Wildlife Art I and II,** *and* **The Birds of Michigan,** *among other books. He also illustrated* **The Legend of Sleeping Bear,** *Michigan's Official State Children's book, as well as* **The Legend of Mackinac Island.** *He was the illustrator on Mario Cuomo's children's book titled* **The Blue Spruce.** *He teaches painting classes and travels to schools throughout the state. His painting of wood storks in the 1999 Leigh Yawkey Woodson Birds in Art Exhibition marked his twelfth inclusion in the international competition.*

F rom a journal that I kept of my visit:

June 13: It was an exciting day that showed why wilderness areas are so important. I had hauled my gear up hill nearly two miles to the top of Lookout Louise, one of the island's highest points. When I reached the top I just stood and dropped everything—the view of Duncan Bay and the Canadian shorelines was tremendous. Suddenly I heard a deep WHOOSH WHOOSH and a golden eagle with at least a six-foot wing span took off from right above me and disappeared over the ledge. A few minutes later it soared past without moving a feather. It was so close we looked each other in the eye. And if that wasn't enough of a thrill, a peregrine falcon also swooped by, forty minutes later, less than twenty feet away. I could hardly believe it. It's truly their place, not ours. You have a better sense of how it may have been centuries ago. The wildlife is right there—right in front of you.

June 17: Finally after eight days of blue skies and sunshine, a thunderstorm shook the cabin during the night. It rained so hard, water leaked through the cabin roof. It's nine o'clock and the waves on the lake must be ten feet tall. It's cold, rainy, and very windy. I asked for it, I got it, but now I don't know if I want it. The lake is very impressive now, white caps everywhere, waves crashing into rocks; places where I was standing yesterday are now under water. I went out and did three paintings during the storm, weighing my easel down with rocks.

June 26: Paintings are hanging everywhere. At the end of each day, I take the finished canvases off the stretcher bars and tack them to the cabin wall to dry. In the evening before dark, I stretch the next day's canvases, brush them with a base or background paint, lay out paint tubes, and clean and sort my brushes. The solitude of this place is the most appealing thing about Isle Royale. I have never painted uninterrupted this much in my life. It was an opportunity of a lifetime and a challenge to transfer such overpowering landscapes to canvas.

The Rock

oil on canvas

16″ × 24″

Scoville Point

oil on canvas

16″ × 24″

1993

Judith Corning

ABOUT THE ARTIST

Judith Corning grew up in Wisconsin and, as a child, spent summer vacations in northern Wisconsin, Michigan, and Minnesota, often on the shores of Lake Superior and sometimes in sight of Isle Royale. She earned a B.S. at the University of Wisconsin at Madison and, after moving to northern California and having a family, began to study art at Laney Junior College and at California College of Arts and Crafts, where she acquired both B.F.A. and M.F.A. degrees.

She was an artist-in-residence on Isle Royale in both 1993 and 1996, and in addition to oil paintings produced one set of prints. "On my second residency I drew an etching on site. I expected the drawing to be less determined by the weather than would be a painting. However, if I left out color in expressing Isle Royale, my sense of the place would be sadly lacking. Isle Royale is filled with lush color of immense variety."

46

The Dassler cabin perches on a small rocky tongue which extends into Lake Superior. Often it is utterly silent there. On Isle Royale frequently the only sounds to be heard in the woods are the plaintive sounds of the white throated sparrows, and the loons in Tobin Harbor when you are lucky.

The day after we arrived, I hauled my painting materials out to the rocks and started to paint. I work slowly so when I stopped some hours later, I planned to resume working the next day and as many next days as I needed to complete the piece. However, the next day the weather was entirely different. So were the lighting and the shadows and, seemingly, everything else. Well, I thought, I'll just have to wait another day or two until the weather conditions repeat Day One. It didn't take long to realize that conditions were never going to repeat Day One.

I hadn't particularly considered weather prior to my first residency because I hadn't painted in a place where the weather changed so fast nor where the weather affected the scene so intensely. This provided a springboard for me to try other than "sunny weather" paintings. My first demonstration painting on the island occurred on an icy sleety foggy morning on the dock at Rock Harbor. I had to head for the laundry room in order to thaw my fingers from time to time. That demonstration painting was my first "fog painting." Inevitably I've done more since then. Atmosphere made its entry into my work. In addition, since becoming weather aware, I've courted it whenever possible. On the island, it is possible to run through our whole year in a week.

On one of our island boat forays, I talked to a woman whose family has been on Isle Royale for some generations. She had returned to enjoy the island and said a major part of what she had been doing was sleeping. I also slept a great deal on Isle Royale. Sleeping in no way implies boredom or lack of things to do; it connotes, rather, the sense of sinking into the restfulness and oneness that seems to pervade the very air, land and surrounding water of Isle Royale even as each day provides a unique landscape to please the eye.

I Know Where the White-Throated Sparrow Sings

oil

22¹/₄″ × 53¹/₂″

Maple Forest, Windigo

oil

18³/₄″ × 29″

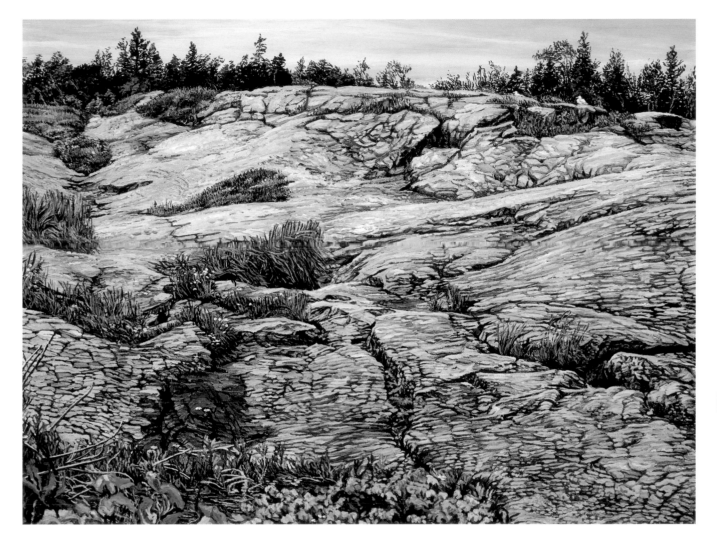

Rocks at Scoville Point

oil

17″ × 23″

Louis Jenkins

ABOUT THE ARTIST

Louis Jenkins' poems have been published in such literary magazines as American Poetry Review *(selected by James Wright),* Boston Review, Gettysburg Review, Kenyon Review, Paris Review, Poetry East, *and* Virginia Quarterly Review. *They also have been included in such anthologies as* Literature: The Evolving Canon *and* The Rag and Bone Shop of the Heart. *Among his books of poetry are* An Almost Human Gesture *(Eighties Press and Ally Press, 1987),* All Tangled Up With the Living *(Nineties Press, 1991),* Nice Fish: New and Selected Prose Poems *(Holy Cow! Press, 1995), which won the 1995 Minnesota Book Award for poetry, and* Just Above Water *(Holy Cow! Press, 1997). Louis Jenkins has read his poetry on Garrison Keillor's* Prairie Home Companion. *His reading as one of the featured poets at the 1996 Geraldine R. Dodge Poetry Festival was included in Poetry Heaven, a program which aired on public television in 1998.*

He lives in Duluth, Minnesota.

I had a marvelous residency on Isle Royale. Unlike some visitors I was lucky enough to have really fine weather during my entire two week stay. Because I was on the island in August and because of the view that Scoville Point affords I was able to witness the incredible display of the Perseid meteor showers almost every night. During the day there was hiking, fishing and, of course, plenty of time to write.

I don't know that the essential nature of my writing was changed by my stay on Isle Royale, but it was certainly enhanced, put in perspective. The Isle Royale experience has now become a permanent part of my psychic landscape. The beauty, the primal water and rock nature of the island, will, I have no doubt, continue to affect my writing for the rest of my life.

The Waves

The east wind has risen today and the waves rise up. Praise to all rising up! To the life that seemed might never return after so many days of dead calm. The wind sends wave after wave scudding toward the shore where the ragged grass clings to the rock. Waves. I recognize some of them. They lift from the void, white-haired but determined, as if each had a purpose, a private destiny, some- place to go (brunch? a board meeting?). Once the savior walked across the water to give each wave, personally, a hand up. Perhaps he is returning even now, but the road to the shore is long, long . . . The waves break and fall face forward, losing touch, losing credibility, losing all pretense of dignity.

The Fishing Lure

I've spent a great deal of my life fretting over things that most people wouldn't waste their time on. Trying to explain something I haven't a clue about. It's given me that worried look, that wide-eyed, staring look. The look that wild animals sometimes have, deer for instance, trying to make sense of the situation: "What *is* that?" Motionless, transfixed. The same look that's on the face of the fishing lure. Stupidity? Terror? What is the right bait for these conditions? High cirrus clouds, cold front moving in. It's all a trick anyway. What is this thing supposed to be? A minnow? A bug? Gaudy paint and hooks all over. It's like bleached blond hair and bright red lipstick. Nobody *really* believes it. There isn't a way in the world I'd bite on that thing. But I might swim in just a little closer.

The View From Scoville Point

This is not the end, but you can see the end from here. Well, often when you think you have come to the end there is one more thing. Out there are a scattering of islands some thick with spruce and balsam, marshes and bogs. Easy to get bogged down with last minute details. It's better to think of each island as a stepping stone. Flag Island, South Government, North Govern- ment, Merritt Island, and last of all Passage Island with its light, not the light at the end of the tunnel, not the warm encompassing light, just a brief flash and then . . . it comes again. Beyond all are the open waters of the big lake. . . . Each passenger receives a hug, a bouquet of flowers, a small box of candy.

Rick Stevens

ABOUT THE ARTIST

Rick Stevens began his art education as a child, watching his father, a self-taught painter, paint scenes of Michigan rivers and woods. Following two years at Grand Rapids Community College, he enrolled in the illustration program at Kendall School of Design in Grand Rapids, which at that time was limited to commercial art. He transferred to Aquinas College's fine arts program and earned a bachelor's degree, then chose to live and paint in a secluded wooded setting that belonged to his family.

As a student he filled sketchbooks until drawing was second nature, then moved to pastels and oils and developed his own complex techniques using acrylics with drawing materials. "During my Isle Royale residency I used only pastels, but since then have completed several Isle Royale paintings in oils from sketch and slide reference."

He lives and works in Sparta, Michigan.

When I saw a TV feature on the Isle Royale artist-in-residence program, I knew that it was exactly the kind of thing that I wanted to experience, and I was determined that I would go to Isle Royale. I began to research what and where Isle Royale was, talking to people who had been there. The myth of the wild north started coming alive for me, cultivating my imagination before I arrived.

The reality of Isle Royale was not a disappointment. I had the feeling that I was in true wilderness. The landscape is unique, both fragile and severely rugged at the same time. The woods are lush with mosses, the trees colored and textured with lichens. Large boulders softened by thick green carpets of moss add to the look that conjured up the mythical lore of the remote north. One such place is along Hidden Lake on the trail to Lookout Louise. I enjoyed watching moose, fox, beavers, and the sunsets around Hidden Lake and Tobin Harbor. There were some stunning moonlit nights also; from the perch at Dassler cabin there is plenty of water to reflect the light. Loons were plentiful around Tobin Harbor but were very elusive when I attempted to come close in a canoe. However, one evening, braving cold waters, I managed to swim within six feet of one to witness an impressive display as it rose up on its tail, beating its wings.

The unfamiliar Isle Royale landscape was a little overwhelming artistically. I think I have done my best Isle Royale paintings since my residency, after time to assimilate and develop ideas. Since Isle Royale I have been a resident at four other national parks and have gained experience in extracting the unique beauty of each place and incorporating it into my own artistic vision. My aim is to be open to revealing (or imagining) and expressing a spiritual landscape whether in remote wilderness tracts, rural agricultural land, or little pieces of "backyard" nature. I have a romantic sensibility for spiritual landscape that alludes to something beyond what is seen. Isle Royale is a place that I carry with me as an archetype of the wild north.

Reflections on Hidden Lake
oil
17″ × 21″

Sunset, Tobin Harbor

oil

20" × 60"

Robert Root

ABOUT THE ARTIST

Bob Root says that he began writing at the age of eight, after he saw Superman and the Mole Men and created his own derivative super-hero, Tiger Boy; he has written constantly since then. He grew up in Lockport, New York, and has a B.A. in English from State University College at Geneseo and an M.A. and a Ph.D. from the University of Iowa. He has published several books on writing and writers, a non-fiction anthology, and an anthology on the teaching of writing.

From 1980 to 1988 he wrote a weekly essay for a local Michigan public radio station and his essays have been widely published. His writing about Isle Royale includes the book "Time By Moments Steals Away": The 1848 Journal of Ruth Douglass, the essay "Pilgrim and Pioneer" in the anthology Peninsula, and a work-in-progress, Recovering Ruth, from which the excerpt in this book is taken.

I would describe myself as an essayist of place fascinated by intersecting histories—the way natural history, cultural history and personal history interconnect. For example, my essay, "Anasazi," recounts the intersection of the natural landscape, the artifacts and ruins of ancient Native American culture, and my own travels; another essay, "Pilgrim and Pioneer," links Ruth Douglass's time on Isle Royale with my island hiking.

Before my wife and I first came to Isle Royale to visit our daughter, Becky, then working at Rock Harbor Lodge, I had read the journal of Mrs. C. C. Douglass, who had lived on the island from August 1848 to June 1849. For a week we hiked along Rock Harbor to Moskey Basin, up onto the Greenstone Ridge, and back to Daisy Farm, where the Douglasses' mining site had been. I wrote an early draft of the essay weaving together Mrs. Douglass's experience and our backpacking and applied for the Artist-in-Residence program the following year. The 1993 residency gave me time to scour the Mott Island archives, wander the Greenstone Ridge and Tobin Harbor, and write my own journal, the source of several subsequent essays.

Working with Ruth Douglass's journal surfaced all sorts of emotions and memories which led me to contemplate my own life. I have been working on a family memoir, tentatively titled *Locks*, and *Recovering Ruth*, a memoir tracing the discoveries and detective work that went into the research on Ruth Douglass's journal.

In August 1998, supported by a Creative Artist Grant in Nonfiction from ArtServe Michigan and the Michigan Council on Artistic and Cultural Affairs to give workshops on editing family manuscripts and do public readings from Ruth's journal, I came back to Isle Royale. One evening, 150 years to the day after Ruth Douglass left Sault Ste. Marie for Isle Royale, I read from her journal in the amphitheater at Snug Harbor. Everything we know of her personality is embodied in the words of her journal; by the end of the reading Ruth Douglass's spirit was once more on Isle Royale. Part of mine has never left.

"Out looking for insight?" the ranger asked me, glancing at the other ranger behind the counter to see if she heard the joke.

I simply smiled without comment and asked about catching a ride down Rock Harbor to Mott Island. I wondered if some earlier artist-in-residence had started the joke by admitting he or she had been searching for insight. The rangers seemed well versed at describing the resources of campgrounds and the distances of hiking trails, at identifying plant life and animal life, at reciting island history. Insight, however, didn't have an entry in the Sierra Club guide to the North Woods and, even if some of the rangers had stumbled upon it, it would be difficult to direct anyone else to the place where it was certain to be spotted.

Yet I suspect that insight in some form is exactly what artists-in-residence are looking for when they accept the chance to spend two weeks in a cabin on Isle Royale, free to hike and canoe, responsible only for presenting one campground interpretive program a week. We are, after all, not scientists but artists—a tag someone placed on my hiking gear when it was shipped to the island identifies me that way. I suspect we want something more than a picturesque patch of landscape to paint or photograph or provoke a poem. We don't want to merely record; instead, we want to comprehend and to find some way to translate that comprehension into the art forms in which we work.

This was my first time as an artist-in-residence. I wasn't exactly certain what an artist-in-residence does (though I certainly knew what one *not* in residence does). I'd come as an essayist. I mostly wanted to wander and to write, and I expected—hoped—that something would come of that. I'd also come partly as an editor-historian. I needed to do some research on Ruth and Columbus Douglass, who had lived in 1848/49 at the Ransom copper mining location (now Daisy Farm Campground). I wanted to browse the archives on Mott Island and wander around the mine site, just to glean whatever information I could.

Perhaps I presumed that, once I started wandering, I would stumble over all kinds of insights, lying across the trail. But it wasn't going to be as simple as that. After catching one boat ride to Mott Island and another to Daisy Farm Campground, and spending time exploring both, I hiked the seven mile stretch back to Snug Harbor, where I waved at the ranger I'd talked to in the morning, and trudged the final two miles to Scoville Point and my cabin. By the end of the hike my knees ached and my feet throbbed and my brain felt numb. There had been no insight lying around on the trail for me to trip over—I would have noticed, because I was watching the ground for most of the hike.

One day, cabin-bound in the rain, I reread Thoreau's essay, "Walking." It's the essay that begins, "I wish to speak a word for Nature, for absolute freedom and wildness, as contrasted with a freedom and culture merely civil." It's the essay where he declares that "in Wildness is the preservation of the World." On the opening page he discusses the art of walking or "sauntering." He derives the word from those who claimed to be going "a la Sainte Terre," to the Holy Land; thus a saunterer is a "Sainte-Terrer" or Holy-Lander. He also tries out a derivation from "Sans Terre," without land, which in Thoreau's view means without "a particular home, but equally at home everywhere." In the first sense the saunterer is a crusader, or perhaps, less militantly, a pilgrim; in the second, he is comparable to a meandering river, seemingly vagrant but ultimately purposeful. I thought I could at least improve my sauntering while I was on the island.

* * *

One morning I canoed across Tobin Harbor and paddled an inner passage on its northern coastline until I reached the Duncan Bay portage. I dragged the canoe a little way up the trail to an out-of-the-way spot, then climbed the easy southern slope to the intersection with the Greenstone Ridge trail and set out west for Mt. Franklin, one of the higher elevations of the ridge.

At first the Greenstone passed through open areas filled with grasses and wild flowers. The ridge is the backbone of the island. As I walked I could gaze into the distance over both north and south shores. Then the forest closed in and the trail passed through a long continuous stretch of heavy undergrowth. I had to pay attention to the trail, not so much because it was treacherous or hard to follow but rather because, with broad thimbleberry leaves up past my waist, I was never certain of my footing. Yet the relative ease and sameness of the trail let me pick my way over it mechanically, and the lack of distraction freed part of my consciousness for rumination. I began thinking about the artist-in-residence presentation I would be giving in a couple of days, and I ended up rehearsing it, imagining it in my head as I hiked. The more I played with it while walking, the more it came together.

By the time I reached Mt. Franklin I was nearly bursting with ideas for the talk. I clambered onto a rocky outcropping a little ways off the trail and sat in the sun for an hour or more, scripting the presentation in my day book. The morning's hike inspired me to take writing on the trail ("sauntering" a la Thoreau) as my theme. As I wrote I felt the sun on my shoulders and the breeze from Lake Superior in my hair, but in the middle of the day on the top of the island I wrote uninterrupted even by birdsong until I knew I'd composed a sentence to end the presentation.

When I stood up on Mt. Franklin and looked off toward the Canadian shoreline, I felt exhilarated to have reached both my destinations, the one on the trail and the one in my script. The feeling kept me aloft on the way back along the trail. As if to confirm my sense of soaring, I spotted a young eagle gliding over the trees to the north above Duncan Bay and watched his flight as long as I could. Shortly after, just as I left the ridge, I located a myrtle warbler by tracing its exuberant song. His music followed me as I descended the trail.

It was already 5:00 P.M. when I launched the canoe again. Despite having been on the trail all day, I wasn't ready to return to the cabin. Instead, I turned the bow toward the head of Tobin Harbor. The island seemed to keep rewarding me for coming to terms with my presentation. Almost immediately I encountered a family of mergansers gliding without apparent effort, and then a family of goldeneyes seeming to skim across the surface. Both times I stopped paddling and let the canoe drift, watching them as unobtrusively as I could.

A little further on I saw a loon ahead of me and heard his loud call; he dove, came up behind me, and called again. I recalled Thoreau playing tag with a loon on Walden Pond and paused in the water. When he submerged again, he seemed to curl and flow into the surface, all fluid silent grace. He emerged in yet another location and let me know where he was although I had already spotted him. I willed myself to turn away from him and scan the opposite direction with my binoculars. Sure enough, a female adult and a young loon were floating in the shadows of a nearby island—the male's antics were merely an attempt to keep me from discovering his offspring. He dove, surfaced, and called again, but I didn't want him to expend his energy on someone as harmless as me and so continued to canoe up the harbor.

As I neared the head of the harbor I remembered Keith Taylor's poem, "Upstream on the Seiche," where he sees the footprints of a wolf in the mud as he drags his canoe toward the water after being beached. I didn't expect to encounter a seiche, to have the water run out from under me after lifting me over the shallows, and I had no hope of discovering wolf tracks, but I wanted to get a sense of the location in the poem. I found a channel into the marsh at the end of the harbor and followed it cautiously. It was narrow and shallow and I soon felt the paddle strike bottom. All at once I was startled by a great thrashing in the reeds, and a great blue heron lifted itself into the air. I watched it go deeper into the marsh and thought that I'd gone deep enough. I turned around before I startled a moose.

Having come up the north shore I headed back down the south side of the harbor, taking the channels between islands when I could. In one channel two white blurs in the trees materialized into a pair of peregrine falcons taking flight; hardly had I turned around from watching them disappear into the distance behind me when I saw a belted kingfisher in the trees opposite where the falcons had been.

By now it was early evening, the sun still high but lowering into the west to illuminate the sky from below. The waters of Tobin Harbor were calm. As I glided into the center of the harbor I realized that I could no longer see into the water. The smooth surface reflected only rich blue sky and powdery white clouds. I could see all the way down the harbor, and I had an uninterrupted view clear to the horizon with sky above and an almost perfect mirror image below. Even close by the canoe, to the eye the lake had become sky.

The canoe drifted across sky; a seagull flew upside down beneath me, and higher above—or deeper below—a cormorant crossed the harbor. For a long time I kept the canoe on course for the distant straight line where sky and mirror image met, hearing only the distant tremolo of a loon, the cry of a gull, the splashing of my paddle, otherwise soundless, solitary, floating down the center of the sky. It was as if I were in flight, gliding with the effortless grace of the eagle, the falcon, as if I were flying through water silent and buoyant as a merganser or a loon. I felt as if I were the only person on the planet, canoeing home down the center of the sky, overwhelmed by the gift the island had given me.

I'd been canoeing about three hours non-stop so I landed at the seaplane dock and stretched my legs by walking along the marina. When I launched the canoe again, the channel was darkening, the surface overshadowed by the trees on the islands I passed. I missed the feeling of canoeing the sky and wished I had kept going as long as I could until the sky disappeared from the water. Suddenly, ahead of me, I spotted movement in the water and slowed the canoe to watch a beaver crossing from the peninsula toward Minong Island. He slapped the water and dove and I didn't see him again. Below the cabin I beached the canoe and clambered up the path to the bluff. From the top of the trail, I saw the two mergansers gliding across the cove on the other side of the promontory. For a moment I watched them with weary pleasure, then I realized that a red fox was standing on the beach, looking up at me. When he saw my gaze turn to him he lingered a moment more, as if giving me time to start moving again, then nonchalantly went up the trail from the beach and disappeared into the woods.

After supper I slid the canoe back into the water and paddled across to Minong Island, where Mary Anderson and her family were staying in the Wolbrink cabin. When I told them about canoeing the sky, her husband, John, a kayaker, told me he had had a similar experience once with the Milky Way. Crossing from shadows into calm open water on a cloudless, moonless night, he saw sky and lake merge in a seamless sheet of stars, dipped his paddles into the stars, brushed stars aside to pull his kayak through the water. When I crossed the channel again in the dark, I only saw a few stars and the distant gleam of the Passage Island Lighthouse. I thought of John Anderson kayaking the Milky Way, remembered myself canoeing the sky. I felt charged with an almost mystical fervor, as if somehow a benevolent Spirit of the Island had been guiding me all day long.

* * *

No one asked me about insight in the days that followed, but by then I knew it was the wrong question anyway. I wasn't looking for a way to understand the island but rather for a way to connect with it, become part of it. This connection isn't something you find, but rather something that finds you. You can't go out on the trail and get it; instead you have to be prepared to receive it. Deliberately searching for insight activates all the barriers of self-consciousness and intellectuality that separate you from the natural world; it closes down your instincts, your intuitions, your receptors. You achieve connection not by aggressive search and seizure but by passive openness and acceptance.

So perhaps I located an insight after all. The insight is the possibility of connection. The connection, though, only comes by canoeing the sky.

1994

Gendron Jensen

ABOUT THE ARTIST

Gendron Jensen was born in River Falls, Wisconsin and studied at the University of Minnesota and St. Benedict's Abbey, Benet Lake, Wisconsin. He is entirely self-taught with no formal art education. He did not start drawing until age 26, but he traces his bond with nature to his childhood.

His first public exhibition was in 1971, at St. Olaf College, Northfield, Minnesota, and his first commercial gallery exhibit was the following year, at Galerie le chat Bernard in Chicago. He exhibited for the first time in Europe in 1984, at the Galerie Bernard Letu in Geneva, Switzerland. He has completed over one thousand five hundred drawings, many in series and monumental in scale. His drawings can be found in collections of such museums as Minneapolis' Walker Art Center and the Los Angeles County Museum of Art.

Some word-glimpses from my sojourn:

A raging wind pulled thundering waves whose spindrifts shot fully ten feet above the high basalt cliffs on Scoville Point. We nestled within our thin-framed cabin, hugging away the chilled droning night which followed.

Beyond the cliffs, ravens uttering throaty, airborne proclamations, whished out from and in to the doorless mists.

Passing over and among boulders, the clear waters of Lake Superior welcomed gazings into their depths. The canoe flew silently, like a great bird bearing us above an undulating shadow cast far below on the rolling bottom of Tobin Harbor.

In thumping hush of first light, the great bull moose bore his ears close around the cabin, peering in at our dark, excited windows.

I relished the predawn light over Edwards Island. The slightest of breezes took it in, playing out intricate patterns of the water's surface.

Hiking alone over windfalls in from Merritt Lane, I swooned at site of wolf-killed moose, whose deathly fern-clad arena was widely carpeted with ghostly hair. All else but broken shoulder blade and part of one leg had gone elsewhere.

The June nights spun loon calls threading back along the rocky shorelines. Out of this, while I slumbered, my darling, Christine, did wakefully hear one wolf singing.

Ahead of the filling moon that ruled most of our island sojourn, we bundled outside into wee hours of one shimmering night, greeted by the northern lights.

Beside woodland trail, the russet moose calf slowly rose blinkingly, summoned away by a mother's nostrilled warnings. Meanwhile, nearby, tiny magenta orchids seemed set about by courtly throngs of Canada dogwoods, festooning the forest floor.

Isle Royale
pencil on paper
14½″ × 23″

Alain Briot

ABOUT THE ARTIST

Born in Paris, France, Alain Briot received his original training at the Academie des Beaux Arts in Paris where he studied painting and drawing. He later studied photography and digital imaging. After moving to the United States in 1986 Briot focused his work on representations of the American landscape in the National Parks and other protected areas. He earned his bachelor's and master's degrees from Northern Arizona University in Flagstaff, Arizona, and later worked on his Ph.D. at Michigan Technological University in Houghton.

Briot now lives in Chinle, Arizona, where his landscape work centers on representations of the American West, Grand Canyon National Park, and prehistoric Native American Rock Art (petroglyphs and pictographs). In 1998 he received the Oliver Award for excellence in rock art photography from the American Rock Art Research Association (ARARA). His work is collected worldwide. It can be seen on the World Wide Web at www.nbn.com/~abstudio.

How does one represent nature? This question was very much part of my experience as Isle Royale Artist-in-Residence. I had just started working with digital photography and was eager to explore its possibilities. Isle Royale offered the perfect location to try to combine photographs. The island was home to a combination of elements which could not easily be captured in a single image. For example, to successfully capture a scene in which a wolf and a moose are interacting in the Isle Royale landscape a photographer would either have to be extremely fortunate or spend much more than a two week residency. I saw this interaction as central to my vision of Isle Royale. Digital imaging allowed me to capture isolated elements of a pre-visualized image and assemble them into a single image once I was back in my studio on the mainland.

I used traditional cameras and shot about one hundred rolls of film, knowing that more was better. I shot landscapes and details. Once back to the mainland I had my films developed, selected approximately one hundred photographs to scan (digitize), and then imported the scans on my computer.

With each image I sought to explore one of the experiences I had while on Isle Royale: the vivid colors of the wood lilies in the midst of so much greenness; the importance of a canoe in the watery expanse of lakes, channels and rivers; the surprise encounter of a moose around a bend in the path; the beauty and history of a lighthouse in a landscape pretty much left to itself; the deadly but ancestral interaction of moose and wolves. I decided to enhance each original photograph in some way so that the completed series would consist of images that are more than photographs. Often, I combined several photographs to create an electronic collage.

My Isle Royale residency allowed me to explore some of the possibilities offered by digital imaging while living on an island where life had remained simple and primeval. Traditionally, landscape artists have sought new tools to express their vision. I see my work as fitting into this tradition while attempting to push the envelope a little bit further.

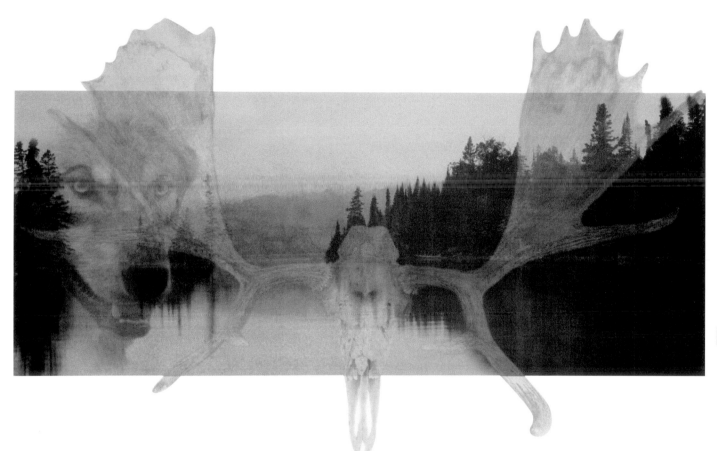

65

Moose, Wolf, and Isle Royale Landscape
digitally enhanced photograph
20″ × 32″

Wood Lilies

digitally enhanced photograph

20″ × 28″

Antler and Moose

digitally enhanced photograph

20″ × 30″

Gregory I. McHuron

ABOUT THE ARTIST

Gregory I. McHuron was born in Syracuse, New York and grew up in Colorado, Wyoming, Alaska, and California. He graduated from Oregon State University in 1968 with a Bachelor's Degree in Art and a background in Forestry and Fisheries and Wildlife. In 1973 he moved to the Jackson, Wyoming, area where he works primarily in oils and watercolors, emphasizing wildlife and landscapes as subject matter.

McHuron was elected to membership in the Society of Animal Artists in 1979 and has participated in SAA shows in New York, Philadelphia, Denver, Cleveland, San Francisco, and Vermont. He has also exhibited in national shows with the Nature Conservancy and Ducks Unlimited, as well as many others. He was the winner of the Old West Museum Award of Excellence in 1984 and the Wyoming Wildlife Federation Stamp Award in 1985 and his work is included in public and private collections in the United States, Canada, and Australia.

I prefer painting on location as much as possible because the drama and excitement which occurs all around me is difficult to recreate in a studio environment. When I paint these rapidly changing scenes, I try to put into each of them the feelings and excitement I felt while watching the scene unfold. If I can capture that particular feeling, then I know that those viewing my works will come to feel some of the emotions and excitement that motivated my wanting to record this particular fleeting moment.

Isle Royale is a wonderful place to step back in time, reflect, and learn about oneself. My main intent in going to Isle Royale was to study how light was affected by being close to a large body of water, as well as being close to sea level, because I live in the mountains of Wyoming at 6700 ft., with very thin atmosphere. I was most fortunate in having the opportunity to be on the island on two separate occasions, which allowed me to build on my first experiences and observations.

The Dassler cabin is situated in a perfect location that affords an extended view of the north end of the island and is isolated enough for artists to be alone for extended periods of time with our thoughts and our work. Travel by canoe and by foot allows us to really slow down and enter the rhythm of the island.

The immediate influence on my work was a change in the temperature of my palette as the light and shadows tend to be much warmer on Isle Royale than what I was used to. Due to the humidity and different flora, the temperature changes required me to sharpen my powers of observation, to think about how and why the light is affected as it strikes various objects and surfaces.

What the long-term influences will be, who knows? I am sure some will be dramatic while others will be subtle—either way they will be ongoing. Would I return? In a heartbeat—in order to paint with more knowledge and emotion rather than thought.

Retired

oil on canvas

16″ × 22″

Welcoming Committee

oil on canvas

16″ × 30″

Rock Harbor Lighthouse

oil on canvas

16″ × 30″

Diane Canfield Bywaters

ABOUT THE ARTIST

Diane Canfield Bywaters has been painting for more than twenty years. Her paintings are displayed in numerous corporate and private collections. She has painted on location in France and Italy and throughout the United States and has been selected as artist-in-residence in a dozen programs, including seven at U.S. National Parks.

Diane has a B.F.A. from the University of Kansas in Lawrence, Kansas, and an M.F.A. from Washington University in St. Louis, Missouri. An experienced arts educator, she has taught at DePauw University in Greencastle, Indiana, and Columbus College of Art and Design in Columbus, Ohio, and presently is a Professor of Art at the University of Wisconsin—Stevens Point, where she has taught drawing, life drawing, painting and color theory. In 1992, she received the University of Wisconsin—Stevens Point's Excellence in Teaching Award and, in 1997, its Scholar Award for her extensive painting exhibition record.

72

My Isle Royale artist's residency was my first time as a National Park Artist-in-Residence. It was such an inspiration to me that it led me to others at Acadia National Park in Maine, Colorado's Rocky Mountain National Park, Arkansas' Buffalo National River, Hawaii's Volcanoes National Park, Indiana National Sand Dunes, and Apostle Islands National Lakeshore. It also inspired me to return two years later to Isle Royale as a tourist. My work concentrates on *en plein air* (a French expression meaning working out-of-doors rather than working in the studio) landscape painting. At Isle Royale, I enjoyed the power of the great lake and the closeness of nature (though at times it kept me awake at night—the little rodents—at least I was hoping they were little—gnawing on the turn-of-the-century cabin.)

I awoke daily to visual inspiration that would fill my day. For example, mist would be rising from the treetops for a mysterious feeling that I attempted to capture. Other days it would be clear and clean and invigorating, and still other days would be aggressively windy (and I would struggle to keep the easel and the painting from going over a cliff). Some days there would be all of those conditions. The excitement of visually capturing this constantly changing environment kept me content. I grew up camping, so though the park is known for its primitive conditions I found the experience totally pleasant and highly productive. I painted over a dozen paintings, gave two lectures to park visitors, and still had time for hiking. I've been told by personnel at other parks that I was selected for their residency programs because they knew, if I could handle Isle Royale, I could handle their parks. Thus, my further success at U.S. National Park residencies was due to my experience at Isle Royale. I returned to Isle Royale with my fishing gear and painting gear two years later as a tourist. Portaging a canoe, primitive camping, fishing for northern pike (my largest: 37″) proved to be exhausting but the land, water, and wildlife restored my soul again.

untitled

oil

8″ × 16″

James Armstrong

ABOUT THE ARTIST

James Armstrong first saw Lake Superior in 1969 on a family vacation, and he has been fascinated with it ever since. He grew up in Kalamazoo, Michigan, where he earned an M.F.A. from Western Michigan University. Armstrong has a Ph.D. in American literature from Boston University and he currently teaches English and creative writing at Winona State University in Winona, Minnesota, where he lives with his wife and two daughters. His book of poetry, **Monument in a Summer Hat,** *was published in 1999 by New Issues Press. He has been the recipient of a PEN-New England Discovery Award and an Illinois Arts Council Fellowship in Poetry.*

From my journal for July 20, 1994:

> *I was tired today—too much going on in my life. All this silence makes the tension come seeping out of every joint where it has been stored up for so long. I slept and had dreams which I can't now recall. The sound of waves fills the cabin and the sun has come out to reveal the sparkling lake and the many islands around us—the light is that peculiar crystalline northern light. I am very pleased by the sudden simplicity of things here—water fetched in a pail, fire kindled on the hearth, candlelight at night. Back to the beginnings of words, and of metaphors.*

The usual purpose of an artist's colony is to provide a time free of distractions—in most such places, meals are provided, and studio space, and one is kept far away from the noise and rush of daily life. The natural beauty of the location—usually these colonies are located on rural estates or in remote communities—is secondary to the main purpose, which is ridding the artist of all excuses for not getting down to the task at hand.

Coming to Isle Royale is not like that—one of the qualifying criteria for applicants is the ability to survive in a wilderness setting. No helpful factotum is likely to appear at one's cabin door with lunch in a hamper. In fact, the artist has to pack his or her own lunch—all his or her prospective lunches for two weeks, as well as all dinners and breakfasts and snacks. What Isle Royale offers is not a respite or a retreat, but a full charge directly into a *subject*—thus one's experience there is concerned with the primary rather than the secondary or tertiary stages of artistic production. The island offers itself as content, and I found that whatever I was doing—observing a moose feeding, chopping the day's firewood, or doing the dishes by candlelight—I was gathering material. This represented a pleasing return to a kind of integrated life, one in which I did not have to compartmentalize the various activities I live by. I found that very inspiring—it was as if the simplest act could regain its mythic or symbolic level, and thus physical labor could be enjoyable again, as life's elemental quality began to show itself.

BRIGHT STAR

I'm sluicing the greasy flatware and handling
the camp mugs with rubber gloves, thinking
of Keats' cold hermit, above a human shore—
his metaphor for the star
which kindles now among the shaking poplar-leaves
out this window, steadfast as the dayblush
wanes. I know where a warbler stirs on her cup
of needles and tinder, packthread and birchfluff,
she is small and dutiful enough.
I know where a lone goosander is fishing late in the inlet
and pecks diffidently at an inverted moon—
but the evening will not be domestic.
The pink museum of the fireweed is closing up,
they are locking the exhibits.

GEOLOGY

All day, all day, reading:
porphyrite, trap rock, felsite, rose-
quartz and prehnite, the uplift of sequences,
subsidence, dip and anti-dip, crazy fractures—
seams of red fire,
the matriarchal on-slosh.
The era of bony fishes and non-bony fishes,
horsetail rushes and proto-crocodiles;
above silted-up bays,
the pulsing wings of a Carboniferous dragonfly—
then the clean break. The great block-plow of the glacier
glittering, edging and backing, leaving the world-ribs
flensed and glistening,
a wilderness of blue gravel and braided outflow.

Canadian Broadcast

I was 25 when I first came into this
secular light, and its astringent cleanliness:
away with the old idols, their quaint shadows,
the fear in earnest faces. Away with
the Revised Standard Bible, the banged drum
of progress, the notion of human hope.
Now the portable radio beside the sink is playing
a Bach piece, it's sad and formal
and I have a vision of the composer's kind disappointment,
his face bending over the lined sheet, with all its little notes—
I can see how the longing for order is always predicting
his work, but never consoling him,
though we are consoled.
For a moment we are consoled.

Constellations

Is there a religious happiness
in the twilight that deepens beyond the inlet,
that infinite picture,
the border of dark on dark?
The pewter stars are faded and childlike
in the day's mausoleum, but night brings them out
on schedule. The sun merely glanced at them,
the night knows better, knows there is an order
in looking at one thing after another:
an act that connects, so we can't think of things after
except as figures, as furniture, as childhood's Monopoly tokens
grown mythically larger:
the boot, the ship, the car.
The harp, the cup, the crown.

James Armstrong: from SCOVILLE POINT FLOW

1995

ISLE ROYALE ARTISTS IN RESIDENCE 1991-1998

Melanie Parke

ABOUT THE ARTIST

Melanie Parke is a visual artist/instructor/organizer. She was born and raised on a small farm near Indianapolis where her parents still reside. Melanie received her B.F.A. from the School of the Art Institute of Chicago in 1989.

Inspired by both the Yosemite and Isle Royale residency programs, Melanie proposed and cooperatively established the Sleeping Bear Dunes Artist in Residence Program in 1992. In 1995, she formally proposed over thirty new residency programs in national parks. The proposals helped to establish six new programs the next year and set fire to a wave of enthusiasm for more programs to come.

In 1997, Melanie moved from Leelanau County to an old, abandoned railroad town called Chief, Michigan. She bought a spacious, one hundred year old country store, which she has transformed into a classroom, home, studio, and on occasion, concert hall.

CeCe Chatfield, friend and painter, arrived for a short stay during my residency. Her baggage was overstuffed with bountiful new rations of granola, fresh vegetables and herbs from her garden, and, for balance, beer and chocolate. Staying in the adjacent cabin, she woke each morning to make us cowboy coffee and toast in a black iron skillet. To this day, the smell romantically transports me back to Tobin Harbor. Together, we paddled and hiked for greater distances than I would have gone by myself. With her company, those were splendid days. I felt the words that Darwin entered in his journal upon first seeing Brazil: "I can only add rapture to rapture."

Alone, however, I often felt spooked. My most adventurous outing was when I took a canoe solo across Tobin Harbor to camp a few nights near Lookout Louise. Along with tent, sleeping bag and cooking gear, I loaded my paint box on top of my pack. Custom made for the Isle Royale residency, my paintbox was designed to slide five wet 8″ × 12″ painting panels into grooves, with one wide slot for a loaded palette. Then through side loops, the box was strapped securely on top of my pack. I set up my easel at Lookout Louise and for the next few days only had to simply shift my weight for a slightly different and expanded perspective. Because weather is so unpredictable, I always feel great urgency while painting outside, but it isn't for the often misconceived idea of "capturing the moment." To the contrary, painting for me is about the passing of time, being there long enough for a conversation, an intimacy, and a lasting recollection.

When I paddled solo far from the cabin in Tobin Harbor, I was a little shaken and a lot humbled. The inner stew of thrill and fear jarred me into becoming raptly present yet willing to remain constantly vulnerable. Alone, I felt that the hand of unknown experience that beckons one on seemed bigger, and the life that spread out before me seemed utterly expanded into new realms.

That got into the brushwork.

That only paint could express for me.

To be given a canoe and a cabin on Isle Royale and to be allowed the passage of time was to be given the most sterling opportunity for joy.

Scoville to Rock Harbor

oil on canvas

16″ × 24″

Lookout Louise I

oil on wood

8″ × 12″

Scoville to Edwards

oil on board

8″ × 12″

Gerald Korte

ABOUT THE ARTIST

Gerald Korte remembers his beginnings as an artist. "For my fourth or fifth birthday, I received a set of pan watercolors as a gift. I then needed a surface to paint on. My search ended when I found a smooth board that was the side of an orange crate. The completed painting, the smiles and compliments from my parents and relatives, made me feel good. This excitement resulted in the beginning of my lifelong adventure in art." After high school graduation he enlisted in the Navy. In the Eleventh Naval District Fine Arts exhibition he received an award for a pen and ink sketch and best of show award for a watercolor. In college, his areas of concentration were art education and biology. Eventually he achieved a master's degree and a doctorate in art education. His teaching experience consists of eight years at all educational levels and twenty-five years at St. Cloud State University at the rank of Professor.

82

Isle Royale overwhelmed me. The lake action, wind through the trees, night actions and day activities and the unique wildlife of the island created lasting impressions. The themes of my paintings reflect personal experiences; in my approach I seek out the pulse of the moment rather than generalities. It is also my goal to leave enough unsaid in order to enable the spectator to participate by supplying the missing ingredients in the form of a recalled encounter, thereby also living the moment. I hesitate to say that I paint "things" but rather I paint the essence of experiences remembered or fulfilled.

The following brief activities will provide an untold number of paintings and sketches:

> One evening, about sunset we quietly canoe along the shore back towards our cabin from Hidden lake. Suddenly Jane whispers, "Moose." A magnificent bull moose is watching us while he meanders along the shore. In an impulsive reaction I give out with a low grunt. The moose answers and in a short while I try it again. Wow, we are communicating, except I suddenly remember—this is the moose rutting season and I am not sure if I am considered a friend or a foe.

> The first evening alone, Scoville Point explodes with strong northeast winds and drenching rains. The propane lantern helps to make the onslaught bearable. Except for chilly nights, the days are pleasant and comfortable. I now enter all day and night sessions in a frenzied painting tempo and establish about twenty-five "starts" that I will work on in my home studio.

> The fall season is in full bloom on the Isle. This is a favorite season for me. Flower colors richly enhanced by the clear skies and sunlight. Migrating birds rest in the perch trees near the cabin and then leave. Hundreds of cormorants herd the fish to shallow shoreline pools to provide the food they need to fly south.

Moose Wallow
watercolor
18″ × 24″

Scoville Point

pen & ink

11″ × 13″

1996

Lee Dassler

ABOUT THE ARTIST

Born in St. Louis, Lee Dassler now lives in Otisfield, Maine, where she is executive director of an historic vernacular garden. Her degrees in Theatre Arts from Wells College and Architectural Preservation from Columbia University allowed her to travel around the world performing and restoring/documenting historic structures.

She has been traveling with a camera in tow since she graduated from high school. "Always there are glimpses of structure, buildings, built objects, unintentional compositions in my slides. The spontaneous theater sets that form the backdrops of our lives." Her fascination with materials and history guided her towards preservation. She worked as a conservator, recording evidence, analyzing material culture, documenting and restoring deteriorated architectural elements. "I have spent the last three years of my life helping to save an endangered landscape in western Maine. That need, my need to preserve and honor the built environment, comes from Isle Royale."

My artist's residency in Tobin Harbor was part preservation, part art, part conspiracy. My family had been among the first summer families to set up camp in the harbor in the nineteenth century. Like many other summer families, we have been left to balance the public good of the creation of the National Park in the '30s with the private sorrow of losing rights to generations of family tradition. In my own life I have been searching for the source of the shadows, the ghosts of my family's traditions. My actions and my art manifest what was lost and my hope that more remains to be found.

When I proposed to photograph the historic structures in Tobin Harbor, I did not realize that the project would include elements of archaeology. Documenting the standing structures was obvious and awe inspiring. The determination of these families to set up camp in this remote situation, and the determination of the materials of their simple cabins and docks to weather the extraordinary nature Lake Superior hurls at them, is inexplicable. Most often the lake won, but not without a good fight. I searched for and documented traces of human habitation: a charred sawn board overcome with lichen, a cut nail, a bed spring, a strip of rusted metal roofing. The most haunting of these ghosts were the dock cribs: massive and pristine below the water's surface.

The structures in Tobin Harbor, even those still used by their families, have been frozen in time, since the creation of the Park. The families that chose to retain life-leases on their properties did so knowing that their lease would expire within the span of a generation. So in general the structures have been maintained but have escaped renovation. The details of the hardware and materials used to construct the cabins and boathouses reflect another age and another approach to life: paced, practical, and yet not without poetry. Even their interior gadgets and household objects reflect the convenience of the early twentieth century. Tobin Harbor is a window to another time, a window that is yet private and deserving of respect. Someday when the story is fully public these photographs will flush out the pace, elegance and frugal practicality of generations and traditions now gone.

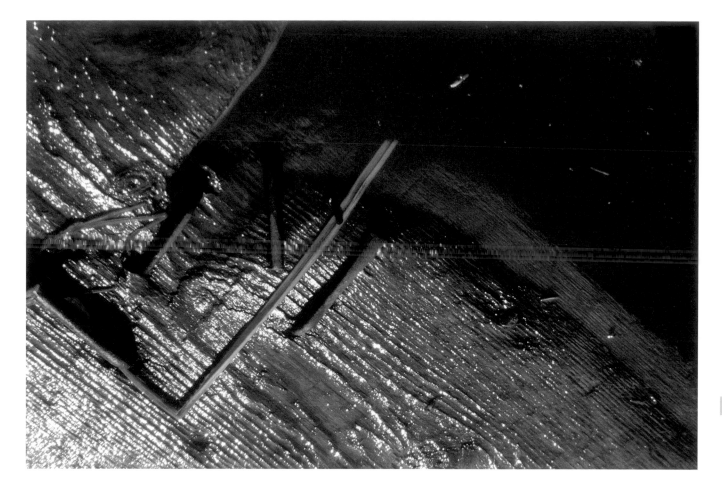

Cut Nail Anderson Dock
photograph
35mm

Edwards Boat Tobins

photograph

35mm

Savage Boat House
photograph
35mm

Tykie Ganz

ABOUT THE ARTIST

The nature paintings of Tykie Ganz have been selected for inclusion in the Arts for the Parks National Competition in 1991, 1992, 1993, and 1996, for work ranging from an Alaskan wolf to birds of Everglades National Park. A painting of a Florida panther was commissioned and published by Lloyd Ellison Graphics, Jupiter, Florida, with all proceeds benefiting the Dreher Park Zoo of West Palm Beach.

Tykie, a resident of Florida, born in Long Island, New York, attended Cortland State University. She has been painting professionally since 1970. An avid wood carver, she has been a founding signature member of Miniature Artists of America since 1985 and is also a member of both the Miniature Art Society of Florida and the Miniature Painters, Sculptors and Carvers Society of Washington, D.C. One of her miniatures is in the permanent collection of the Smithsonian, Washington, D.C.

Tykie Ganz is included in Who's Who of American Women and Who's Who in American Art.

Isle Royale! My most memorable and enchanting experience. I imagined the pioneers as they surveyed the West. Isle Royale was my wilderness. No human foot had trod my ground. My work was begun by the light of dawn and finished by the twilight of darkness. Then and only then I lay in my cocoon and listened to the sounds of night. The waves lapping the rocks below the cabin, the loon's call. How soft, compared to the rush of cars, the wail of sirens, the noise of humanity.

I would awake to the white throated sparrow's familiar song and rush outside. The air was brisk and clean. The master painter had lifted the fog for me to see. From the smallest blade of grass and beautiful wildflowers to the tallest trees; the cliffs weathered by eons of wind and water; the coastal rocks glistening with the splash of waves; a pair of Canada geese at rest on the shore. What I looked for most at Isle Royale—the wolves—I did not see. But their spirit, hidden in my wilderness, was there. My paintings could only try to capture my friends—and try I did. And as I left Isle Royale, I left a part of my spirit with them.

Moose in Tobin Harbor
acrylic
22″ × 28″

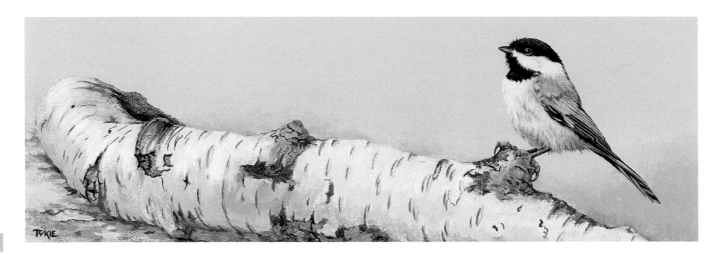

Chickadee

acrylic on canvas

4″ × 12″

Loon and baby

acrylic on canvas

15″ × 30″

Elizabeth Holster

ABOUT THE ARTIST

Elizabeth (Betsy) Holster grew up in Minnesota and spent her summers among the many beautiful small lakes in the northern part of the state.

After high school, she attended the University of Wisconsin at Madison, majoring in wildlife ecology before switching her major to art for her bachelor's degree. She moved to Houghton and enrolled in the School of Forestry at Michigan Technological University, where she met her future husband, an engineering student. After graduation they settled in Misery Bay, near Houghton, built a large log home, and, with their two children, lived there without running water or electricity. "We loved it."

In 1988, they moved to Iron Mountain and she commuted to Northern Michigan University for her master's degree in art. "We have kept our log home in Misery Bay, spending as much time as possible there, where we hope to eventually retire."

Lake Superior has long been my chosen fixation. The Artist-in-Residence program gave me an opportunity to spend almost three weeks focusing entirely on my interest in the lake and its environs. It enabled me to closely observe Isle Royale settings in a wide variety of weather and lighting conditions. I was able to explore the same sites at different times of the day, taking reference photographs that best reflected the ideas and emotions I wished to capture.

One of my friends described "the ultimate Isle Royale experience" as watching an antlered moose swimming from island to island. After they left Isle Royale, I was paddling by myself, deep in thought about this "ultimate experience" and what a shame it was that I wouldn't be able to see it. I was so deep in thought that I almost missed seeing a moose across the channel as he got into the water and swam, with his massive rack held above the water. When he came out on the other shore I allowed myself to drift a bit closer to watch. It was an "ultimate experience".

Where else can a person go hiking and feast on blueberries, strawberries, thimbleberries, and raspberries all on the same day? On the top of Lookout Louise there is a rock formation that seats one person comfortably, with a most stupendous view. We called this the "Queen of the Universe" chair and took turns soaking up the ambience.

The cabin provided by the Park Service has a bench where one can view both the sunrise and the sunset. After spending time at my own Lake Superior home facing west and only seeing sunsets, it was a real treat to be able to see both the beginning *and* the end of the day. It was also a wonderful place to watch the stars.

The time I spent on Isle Royale helped me to clarify what it is I want to say through my work. The in-depth experience made my drawings of the island setting stronger, richer and deeper. I want to use the setting of Lake Superior and the passion I feel for the Lake region to convey a sense of the interconnectedness of all aspects of the natural world. The intricate patterns found within rocks and water are some of the most fascinating natural designs that exist. I want to use these images as my vocabulary for expressing my vision.

Isle Royale Portage
color pencil
36″ × 30″

Reflections

color pencil

26″ × 24″

Merritt Lake
color pencil
28″ × 18″

Richard Schilling

ABOUT THE ARTIST

Richard Schilling's love of watercolor began as a youngster in grade school when he was chosen to receive instruction in the medium at the University of Nebraska on Saturday mornings. Many years later, he graduated from the same university with a degree in dentistry. For the past thirty-five years he has practiced both dentistry and the art of watercolor painting. "I chose dentistry for my livelihood, but art permeates every aspect of my being. The two are partners that travel easily with unusual harmony."

His work as a volunteer in several developing countries and as a ship's dentist has provided him with opportu-nities to paint around the world. Today, this is his consuming interest, and he delights in sharing his knowledge with others in workshops that he teaches.

He says of his experience as an artist-in-residence at Isle Royale National Park, "This experience will always remain one of the highlights in my life." His painting of the Edisen Fishery was chosen one of the top one-hundred paintings in the Academy of Arts for the Parks national traveling exhibition during 1997–1998.

A few notes from my Isle Royale diary:

July 2, Scoville Point: I found the cottage that would be my home for the next three weeks sequestered under pines and birch on a rocky promontory thirty feet above the waters of Tobin Harbor. Inside, the cottage walls and furniture are slightly askew to a plum line, yet they welcome me as a similarly flawed friend. The wavy windowpanes sparkle with jewel-like air inclusions. A skilled stone mason built the fireplace and hewed from a log its decorative mantle. Even though it is now late in the evening, the light is only beginning to fade. It has not been necessary to burn the kerosene lamps. Tomorrow I will explore the island for watercolor subjects.

July 6: I am beginning to bond to the cottage. One must invest time to develop a relationship. It rained most of the day and my only option was to paint a view from the cottage window of spruce and birch trees and the distant islands. It is taking me at least three times as long to paint here as in Colorado due to the humidity which has prolonged the drying time of my watercolor washes. I stand my damp watercolors up to dry, like laundry, towards the warmth of the fire. Such a minor annoyance will not deter me from the excitement of painting the wilderness.

July 9: I hiked to Snug Harbor and arrived just as the M.V. Sandy was casting off for Rock Island Lighthouse and Edisen Fishery. I was greeted at the fishery by a scene that looked much like a movie set. Rotting boat hulls were floating in a sea of wild flowers, and antique implements were scattered in the yard long ago by fishermen whose woven nets have been wound on giant wooden reels. I painted a rendering of the fishery and one of the lighthouse before the Sandy embarked for home.

July 19: The cottage screen door slammed shut this morning as I headed down the path to the outhouse that bore the inscription R.I.P. The sudden intrusive noise frightened a bull moose that had been standing beneath the eaves of the cottage. He thundered down the path narrowly missing me. For days I had seen fresh tracks next to the cottage windows but was unable to catch the window-peeker in the act. It caused me to reflect—who had come to observe whom in this magnificent north woods wilderness?

The Edisen Fishery

watercolor

17″ × 25″

View from Guest Cottage

watercolor

18″ × 22″

1997

Gary Lawless

ABOUT THE ARTIST

Gary Lawless says, "I have always lived in Maine, where, as a child, I felt a great love for the outdoor world—the woods, the rivers, the ocean." In high school he started reading poetry about the natural world and trying to write poetry. In college he focused on East Asian Studies, especially Chinese and Japanese poets. Instead of going to graduate school he went to live at the California home of poet Gary Snyder and worked as his poet's apprentice.

Homesick for Maine, he returned and has lived there ever since. He co-owns a bookstore, runs his own book publishing company (Blackberry Books), writes poetry, and teaches creative writing and environmental literature (currently at Bates College). "I have always felt that poetry is a useful way to bring voices back into the community, so I have led long-term writing programs with Maine's homeless and disabled communities." He has also worked with refugee families and prisoners and has taught in an adult education program for the last six years.

As a writer, I have wanted to explore those places Thoreau called "mossy and moosey"—not only in my native state of Maine but also across North America. I have spent time in Newfoundland, Labrador, Alberta, and Alaska. I have wanted to be where the large mammals were—moose, bear, wolf, caribou. From my reading about wolves, and about moose, I had thought of Isle Royale as a kind of fantasy land, an island surrounded by a great expanse of water, somewhere to the west—a place to dream about, but not a place to actually be. A trip out to Isle Royale had never seemed a possibility until I learned of the Park's Artist-in-Residence Program.

Once on Isle Royale, I wanted to know everything. What the relationship is between moose and wolf and how has this altered the island; what plants were here before the moose and which are endangered; what birds are here, what mushrooms, what butterflies (the pamphlet listing the names of butterflies on Isle Royale is a poem in itself). All of these questions and more brought me to the geology of the island, and the idea of the island rock as a host to other molten rock, to greenstone, to glaciers, copper, caribou, loons, wolves and moose, devilsclub, lily, migrating birds, native Americans, fishermen, tourists. I had to learn about the rock. I had to learn about the plants and animals, about wind, fog, and rain.

I spent most of my days walking or paddling. Only heavy rain or darkness kept me inside the Dassler cabin, but those times gave me a chance to read the field guides and related texts. I went to the ranger talks and on guided boat trips. Each day I had to decide what I wanted to see, what I wanted to explore. Did I want to visit the moose, or look for greenstones, or hang out with the ducks, or look for that newly opened wildflower, or just walk the ridgeline?

As I moved around the island, I tried to bring the island into my head, into my heart. I breathed the air, drank the water, ate the fish and berries, and the island literally became a part of me. I kept the information gained from looking, hearing, smelling, touching, from my contacts with the island, within me—and this information, these images, emotions, sensations, are worked over inside me and come back to the surface as poems. I believe that in this way I will forever carry the island within, as a part of myself, and that my poems are a way of sharing that connection, that conversation, with others.

ISLE ROYALE
a place where the wolves are wanted,
where human beings bring our awkward blessings to
moose bone, wolf scat, loon song.
where we allow ourselves to blossom
among marsh marigold, rock harlequin,
calypso orchid, Labrador tea.
where we peel back layers of fog, moss, rock itself
Inside there is sunlight
Inside there is wolfsong
the light step of the moose,
berries waiting to ripen
where the wind never touches
All this light
at the heart of things.

Nothing but moosetrails in the mist,
today's fog and wind,
trees against sky.
I want to disappear into cloud,
wander my way to sunlight,
follow the moose down
secret trails in the woods
to reach the places where the wolves
rest above the ridges, within us,
where the heart wanders, wild.

water connects with water.
six days with little rain.
the moose is in the swamp.
ducks begin to speak.
We walk the ridgelines
thirsty for everything:
that yellow flower,
that bird overhead.
Without knowing, we drink,
and leave with the island
inside of us.

layer upon layer of leaves settles slowly,
moss growing on top.
layer upon layer of lava flows,
minerals rising to fill the veins.
burned bare ridges and parallel bogs.
as we walk our minds
drop through layer after layer
to host rock:
tough, bare, essential.
the wind can't harm us.
the water, all around,
touches, touches,
waiting for the glacier.

Joe M. Cronan

104

Looking at the progression of work from the summer leading to the Isle Royale artist's residency to now, I see the rough edges of a personal compositional question being raised, tripped over, and smoothed. The question is: How do I engage the photograph? I did not know the question while photographing at Isle Royale. Only after looking at the body of work as it related to how I photographed before and after did I begin see the question and how Isle Royale laid the cornerstone of the answer. I have a quieter, less dramatic approach to the landscape and photography now. Perhaps an excerpt from my journal will help explain.

Sept. 3, 1997

The sun is setting, reflecting off of a lone strung-out cloud over the ridge to the west. A loon is wolf-calling with an occasional answer floating back up the harbor. I am on the bench on the promontory behind the cabin. At the foot of the bluff at my feet Lake Superior becomes Tobin Harbor. In the distance to my right, the northeast, the Passage Island Lighthouse is blinking its warning. On my knee—a mosquito.

This is the first night since we have been here that the evening wind isn't howling. I was going to take a night photograph with colored light, but just couldn't do it. It may be that I'm tired from the day's activity or maybe I don't have anything else to say that way. Maybe I'll start platinum printing.

I slept late today. Lori got up to see the sun rise and make some biscuits. The lake was choppy but started quieting down. We decided to paddle to the end of Tobin Harbor. We paddled into a stiff head wind for four hours and didn't make it. It took us two and a half to make it back with a long stop at the Rock Harbor Visitor Center. We are pretty tired with sore shoulders.

Today was also the day I resigned myself to this part of the island. I will seek inspiration in a short space.

The loons have begun their crazy as a loon call and it is dark.

PS. After a nice cup of hot chocolate we sat out on the bench and watched a meteor shower fall into the aurora borealis.

PPS. The loons are wolf-calling again.

Needles and bark

photograph

14″ × 9¹/₄″

Thimbleberries

photograph

9¹/₄″ × 14″

Wave, Scoville
photograph
9¼″ × 14″

Wanda Zuchowski-Schick

Wanda Zuchowski-Schick says that she has always been an artist. She was raised and still resides in Rossford, in Northwest Ohio, the ninth of fifteen children. She attended Bowling Green State University and graduated with a major in Art Education. She married, started a family, and began teaching art in the Toledo Public School system, where she is still teaching. "As my children were growing, I was more of an art teacher than an artist. My sons David and Brian have cystic fibrosis and their medical care came first. In the summer of 1984, my son David, lost his 14 year battle with cystic fibrosis. His passing created a deep void and a tremendous sadness in my life."

Wanda enrolled in the University of Toledo majoring in printmaking and earning a Masters of Art in Education degree.

Although she works in more than one medium she prefers watercolor and printmaking. A ten-foot oil painting of Isle Royale was exhibited at the Toledo Museum of Art in 1998.

For me, my residency at Isle Royale was a time to rest, explore, plan, contemplate, and heal. After another year of teaching art classes in an inner city high school, I needed the quiet and calm of a remote cabin in the wilderness on an island in the middle of a vast and deep lake. I soon became acutely aware that this island was not quiet. The sounds of nature amplify in the wild.

For five days I talked to not a soul. I hiked the trails and painted with watercolors. I took photographs, sat quietly and just observed. I began a painting with a view of Lake Superior from the Stoll Trail.

The weather went from sunny and warm to foggy, then stormy. On July 2, the winds picked up. Huge waves crashed against the rocks below the cabin, spraying water everywhere. I switched to oils and painted the islands in Tobin Harbor, trying to capture the waves crashing and storm clouds rolling in. My outdoor painting ceased when the winds became severe.

After a week on my own, my son, Dan, arrived. Early the next morning we packed up the canoe. We paddled around Scoville Point into rough Lake Superior waters along the coast of the island towards Rock Harbor. We were close to the lodge when we noticed the tent was not in the canoe. Dan volunteered to be the one to hike back and get the tent. I sat in the canoe and began a new painting. The scene was developing nicely when a wave hit the canoe. My paints, brushes, and painting fell into Lake Superior. The clear water allowed me to fish out each and every watercolor pan and brush, but the painting was ruined.

The waves got higher and the water rougher. The wind was in our faces. We clung to the shoreline. Rock Harbor felt like we were paddling through thick soup and Moskey Basin, mud. We almost quit. But we were determined. Exhausted we pulled into Moskey Basin campground. After that the trip was comparatively easy. We camped and portaged and fished.

Without my son I wouldn't have been able to experience as much of the island that I did. Yet I shall return again because I feel I have missed so much. The visual images stay with me and dominate my work. Isle Royale National Park has been in my classroom, my experience, piles of photographs, slides, and paintings shared with my students.

Isle Royale has become a place that I can go to in my mind when I need a break from the hectic schedule that I have. It helps to calm my soul.

Encounter Along the Stoll Trail

watercolor

21″ × 29″

Marilynn Mallory Brandenburger

ABOUT THE ARTIST

*Marilynn Mallory Branden-
burger says that her work
celebrates American wilderness. To find her subjects,
she travels regularly to
remote places, such as the
national parks, where the
land is still wild and the
natural environment is undis-
turbed by man. "Drawing on
sketches and photographs I
recreate my wilderness
experiences in paint back
home in my studio."*

*Born and raised mostly in
the Midwest, she has lived in
the South for more than thirty
years. She received her B.A.
degree from Tulane University
in New Orleans and her
master's in art education
from Florida Atlantic University in Boca Raton, Florida.
After raising a son and
earning a living in a variety of
administrative positions, she
now works as an artist full-
time, dividing her time
between painting and
teaching. One of her recent
paintings of Isle Royale has
been selected for the 1999
Arts in the Parks Top 100
exhibition. In addition to the
Isle Royale paintings, she
is producing a series on
Glacier Park, where she was
artist-in-residence in 1998,
and on the Smoky Moun-
tains, which are a favorite
weekend retreat.*

When I first arrived on the island, I was full of the nervous energy and concern that's typical of my city life. Very quickly however, the island demanded that I give up all the mental agitation. The enormous quiet that surrounded the cabin forced my mind to relax; the simple chores required for daily living pushed all the goals aside. Because there was no electricity, I had to wake and sleep with the rising and setting of the sun, and so came to love the special beauty of dawn light and the changing phases of the moon. Because there was no agenda, I came to spend each day learning more about the two square miles in which I was living, spending long hours listening to the lake crashing against the cliff edges, observing ducks riding incoming waves, examining tracks left in the rocks by glaciers, noticing how the color of grasshoppers' wings matched the chartreuse of rock moss, selecting pebbles of special texture and beauty to decorate the cabin, following the sun as it tracked its warmth across distant islands, watching the moon spread daggers of light across the lake, and feeling the wind charge the air and trees with energy. I was amazed at how quickly time passed when I was absorbed in these things, how much I came to enjoy the simple pleasures of my own company, and how easily the images I sought for paintings appeared when I was in this state of simple quiet.

I had a sketchbook and camera to provide visual recall, but I needed a tool that could capture the sensory experiences and the feelings. I decided to undertake a daily journal. Every evening I recorded the minutiae of my day: the weather; the comings and goings of animals, birds and people; my activities; my moods, fears, joys, and general musing, both profane and sublime, about what I saw, felt, and painted. Now, more than a year later, I can open the pages of the journal and a flood of memories brings the island back to life.

Now, when I am in other wilderness places searching for images to paint, I use those lessons I learned at Isle Royale: I get quiet and let the wilderness reveal itself to me; then I write. Then, back home, with a wealth of experience and the journal to rekindle it, I can fill my paintings with the same feelings I had when I was in the wilderness.

Moonrise—Scoville Point

color pencil on paper

18″ × 24″

ANOTHER VIEW OF SCOVILLE POINT

Isle Royale sketchbook

ink

8½″ × 11″

SAT AUG 9

THE DASSLER CABIN
THIS IS TO BE MY HOME FOR THE NEXT
TWO WEEKS. PERCHED ON A 50 FT.
CLIFF OVERLOOKING LAKE SUPERIOR,
THE LITTLE CABIN FACES EAST, WELCOM-
ING THE RISING SUN.

A SNUG PLACE: PINE-
PANELED, SMELLING OF WOOD
SMOKE & BALSAM FIR. THREE
ROOMS: THIS SMALL LIVING ROOM,
A TINY BEDROOM, A COMPACT BUT
"EFFICIENT" KITCHEN — THAT IS, WITH A
WORKING STOVE AND REFRIGERATOR. WATER
COMES FROM THE LAKE, BUCKET BY BUCKET.

113

Isle Royale sketchbook

ink and color pencil

11" × 8½"

Sheila Larkin

ABOUT THE ARTIST

Sheila Larkin grew up in an Irish-American household, surrounded by family, music, religion, and scouting. In college she straddled two majors: music and environmental studies. She has degrees in music from the University of Wisconsin and music therapy from the University of Minnesota. She has performed as a solo piano player for fifteen years and co-founded a Celtic band called Brigits Fire. A featured artist on a Narada Productions recording entitled First Light (1996), she is currently recording some of the material she wrote as a result of her residency on Isle Royale. In addition, she has practiced music therapy in a wide variety of settings for over seventeen years. She is presently living in Oconomowoc, Wisconsin, and working as an elementary school counselor in the nearby town of Sullivan.

114

When I arrived on Isle Royale for the first time in July of 1997 I felt great excitement to be there, as I had long heard about the island's pristine wilderness. But, arriving at the cove that harbors the artist's cabin, I was unprepared for the sheer beauty. A ranger took us up to the point in front of the cabin, to the expansive view. Standing there, looking out, he remarked wryly, "If an artist can't get inspired up here, I don't know *where* she could!" It was at that spot on a windy and sunny day, seated at a weathered bench, that I wrote "From A Point of Stone," a song that seemed almost to come out *whole*. From that bench I saw the northern lights and amazing sunsets and heard the rush of gulls and loons above and mergansers below. At the height of that point you share the sky with the birds and can be startled awake in early morning hours by the call of a loon as it wings just over the roof of the cabin. I spent many hours at that bench reading, singing, and taking in the sights and spirit of the place. It is an honored spot.

Honored is a word that well describes my time as artist-in-residence on Isle Royale. It gave me the chance to look into myself (including meeting some fears), acclimate to the rhythms and moods of the lake and island, and feel a joining of art and place. My time on Isle Royale was a highlight in my life. I met wonderful folks, experienced indescribable beauty on a daily basis, and absorbed the essence of the natural environment: the sky, birds, moose, lush forests, mists, thimbleberries, rocks, and, always, the water. That type of absorption forms a pool of experience that I somewhat unconsciously draw from when I create music. I grieved for weeks, even months, after leaving the island, for the sense of place and immersion that I'd felt.

Back in southern Wisconsin I placed photos of the island throughout my home. One of my strongest memories is that of paddling solo up Tobin Harbor, peering into the water as I glided, and shuddering a bit as I clearly viewed huge boulders that lay on the bottom of the harbor many feet below in the ice-cold water. Clarity, strength, complexity, and delicate beauty—these are all qualities of Isle Royale. It has become a part of me, my music, my spirit, and I hope to have a long and deepening connection with the island for years to come.

From a Point of Stone

Music and lyrics by
Sheila Larkin

Music and lyrics © 1997 by Sheila Larkin

1998

Amy E. Arntson

Amy E. Arntson says that her "paintings reflect the qualities of the natural forms and spaces of the Great Lakes region. The body of my recent work is a combination of still life, landscape, and most importantly, paintings of water. As an artist and an educator, I am interested in the relationship between our environment and ourselves. The sense of place that most influences my sensibilities is the Great Lakes region where I grew up and have spent the majority of my career."

118

A Professor of Art at the University of Wisconsin-Whitewater since 1982 and author of **Graphic Design Basics,** *Arntson was born in Frankfort, Michigan. She earned a B.F.A. from Michigan State University and an M.F.A. from University of Wisconsin-Milwaukee. She is an artist, writer and educator. Her lectures and presentations have spanned the globe from New York to London, Beijing to Costa Rica and Peru. Her work has been selected by invitation or jury to be shown in over one hundred group and one person exhibitions and is shown in several galleries in the region.*

It's been many years since I've worked outdoors, sketching with watercolors directly from the subject. Usually I work in my studio with a variety of still life set ups and photographic references. Spending nearly a month at Isle Royale, working outdoors during daylight and by lamplight during the evenings, was a special experience from which I learned and re-learned a great deal.

Evenings were spent reading in front of the fire or painting at the table by kerosene lamplight. Our drinking water was pumped up from Lake Superior, and it gave me special pleasure that my paintings were created using Lake Superior on my brush.

Dawn came with various guises. I often sketched it while sitting on the rocks beneath the cabin, my feet damp, with hot tea beside me. The rock formations and the water became my primary subjects. The rock formations are so beautifully, strongly structured, with brilliant lichen for accent and texture. Drawing them reaffirmed the importance of structure in my compositions. I made a paper viewfinder with a rectangular opening to help me choose what to paint and to block out everything else. I sometimes spent nearly as much time looking through that paper frame as I did on the sketch itself. The act of framing became a metaphor for the process of deciphering and relating to life.

The water held me fascinated. I began by trying to fix it in my mind like a snapshot, frozen. But I couldn't. It was so complex, with ripples and wind and cross currents and eddies. Gradually I began to try to understand the reason for the surface patterns. And then I began to paint it with some conviction. Yes, there are ripples on the ripples. But there are also currents and cross currents caused by land formations that interact on the water's surface with the effect of the winds. To sketch or paint this I had to learn to understand its structure as a sailor might. Kayaking definitely helped. Those wind shadows from the islands are a thing to paint, as well as a place to rest your tired arms.

I re-learned how to see while I worked in my sketchbook, alive to the brilliance of the colors all around me. And my work loosened, my brush trying to catch the lively, ephemeral quality of the days. The hundreds of photographs taken during my stay on the island are the basis for studio work during the winter.

Superior Wave

watercolor

16″ × 17″

Hidden Access

watercolor

19″ × 12″

Super Kayak II
watercolor
12″ × 9″

Deborah Eddy

Isle Royale is one of the most memorable places in my life; I miss it still. The three weeks of my residency, away from everything and everyone I know, concentrating on my art, was a treasure to me. Exploring such a beautiful place intensely, in such a limited period of time, caused heightened awareness. So much can be accomplished in that state.

When I first learned I would be an artist-in-residence, I studied the maps and the literature and believed I could thoroughly explore the entire island while creating a large group of paintings all in my allotted time. Reality, and confusion, struck immediately upon my arrival. I spent the first few days hiking all over my end of the island. I canoed in the cove. I needed to discover the essence of Isle Royale in order to portray it to others. Time was short.

Pushing past some fear, I decided to canoe to the nearest small island. It didn't seem too far away and I could see that it had a landing beach. This trip proved to be a breakthrough. My "discovery" of Smith Island, a miniature version of Isle Royale, clarified my observations of Isle Royale. My first painting was done on Smith Island.

My presentations to park visitors also proved to be invaluable to me. Answering questions posed to me drew out the observed information I had not yet recognized. I realized the most important elements of Isle Royale: the lush forest, the white light, the pervasive rocks and roots, and the yellow-green color all around. All of these represented the visual essence of this place to me. Also, the respect and interest shown by the audience was an honor that continues to support my work.

One surprise of my residency was the rock sculpture/collage that I created on the beach at the bottom of the trail to the cabin. This project started by accident on my first day and finished on my last. It began when I placed a rock, marking the beginning of the trail. I was having trouble finding the trail in the dark and hoped this marker would help me get home. The sculpture grew from that rock, to cover a large section of the beach on either side of the trail. If I had had more time I might have rearranged the entire beach! Creating this work was totally unexpected and thoroughly enjoyable. I'm glad that a part of me was left behind on the shore.

Observation #1 Isle Royale

pastel on paper

6″ × 6″

Observation #4, Smith Island

pastel on paper

12″ × 6″

View from the Cabin, Isle Royale

pastel on paper

9$\frac{1}{2}$″ × 25$\frac{1}{2}$″

Joyce Koskenmaki

My stay at Isle Royale, just prior to my move back to the Upper Peninsula, was a beautiful re-initiation into the landscape that I love. I came with the intent of studying the moose so I could finish a good painting of a moose which would express my feelings about animals and nature. I did manage to spend some time with that majestic being, but fox, rabbit, squirrel, seagull, loon, and ducks also all came to me at some point. At Isle Royale no one can shoot or trap them. They are safe. So in some way that makes my own spirit safe when I am there, connected as we all are with the spirits of wild creatures.

There was intense magic in canoeing at night down Tobin Harbor, the moon keeping us company, loons calling to each other, the horizon disappearing so that it felt as if we were suspended in the sky. The big storm the night before we left gave us a challenge which tested our capacity to trust the universe to take care of us. Huge waves threatened to capsize our fragile vessel, and when we managed to finally make it to land, our relationship to those great forces had changed forever our sense of being.

The many walks down and up the trails, the afternoons sitting in the sun on Scoville Point, drawing with the company of curious seagulls, the thimbleberries renewing themselves for our benefit every day. The times we traded sketches for boat trips to lighthouses and other places we couldn't walk to, the rangers who took care of us with such friendship, the aurora borealis one long night, the ducks who met me every morning and accompanied my sunrise meditations, the fox who came and watched us while we painted—all of these have become part of me forever.

The experience of intense closeness to this protected wilderness has given a new vitality to my work which was not possible when I was living in an urban environment. I have confidence that it will continue.

Island

color pencil on watercolor

11″ × 8½″

Passage Island

ink on paper

11″ × 8½″

Pine tree
color pencil
11" × 8½"

Jennifer Williams

ABOUT THE ARTIST

Jennifer Williams is a faculty member of the art department at the University of Wisconsin-La Crosse, where she teaches painting. She earned her M.F.A. in Painting and Printmaking from Rhode Island School of Design and a B.F.A. in Painting from Indiana University.

Williams began five oil paintings on the island, and returned to her studio to complete them. The properties of oil enable her to "re-experience" the place throughout the working process, allowing the blended hues of landscape to emerge over time.

Easily portable watercolors were a preferred way of capturing the light of a given moment in the several color sketches that Williams worked on at Isle Royale. Still another inspiration was the wonder of the aurora borealis seen for the very first time while on the island; "it was difficult to resist the challenge to express this astounding spectacle of light and mystery." Both watercolor and pastel works fueled by this experience served as studies for larger oils completed later in the studio.

The experience as an artist-in-residence at Isle Royale profoundly affected my work. Continuing to develop work based on this experience has fulfilled a need—the need to return to the island often. I am sure to return to the place physically someday, but in the meantime, simply painting an image of the place doesn't come close to recreating the encounter. It is necessary instead to return to the island in spirit, to recall the experience as completely as possible, with a deeper recollection than images alone can provide. In order for me to do this in my painting I must surround myself not only with photographs of the island but also with my journal, and with the watercolors and drawings I made there. It is most important to activate an awareness of everything the experience meant, an awareness that is best informed by memory.

I was fortunate to share my residency with another artist and friend of mine, Joyce Koskenmaki. We found our sources of inspiration to be similar in many ways, while our visual recording of our experiences reflected our own unique visions. Both of us felt drawn to the enigmatic presence of the distant islands in Tobin Harbor, and it has been interesting to compare our interpretations.

The relationship between realism and abstraction has always intrigued me, and I found a natural synthesis of the two in the study of lichen patterns on the rocks at Isle Royale. These paintings were important links to paintings I had begun before I ever went to the island and are in many ways the most tactile and experiential works I continue to produce. I think of the surface not as a representation of landscape but as landscape itself, even though I am using the traditional medium of oil paint. I conceive of the surface as both map and terrain, full of pattern and texture, and full of the memory of walking the trail.

While I may not continually make paintings that represent Isle Royale directly, my experience of the place will be reflected in my work for a very long time. What has always been present in my work is the suggestion of a deep sense of longing, a human connection to landscape. After all, how can one remember Isle Royale without a profound sense of longing?

Near Dassler Cabin at Dawn

watercolor

5″ × 7″

Northern Lights

oil on canvas

18″ × 54″

George Provost

ABOUT THE ARTIST

George Provost has been photographing the wilderness and printing black and white photographs in Alaska since 1987. Although he has taken some college classes in photography and attended several photography workshops, he is primarily self-taught using the Ansel Adams series of technical books..

Currently he is finishing his eighth year of college and pursuing a master's degree in clinical psychology. His photographs have been exhibited and awarded in over 55 exhibitions in Alaska, Russia, and the lower forty-eight states. The Anchorage Museum of History and Art, the Alaska State Museum in Juneau, and the University of Alaska Fairbanks Museum have his photographs in their permanent collections. He has received two artist's grants from the Alaska State Council of the Arts.
He works with an 8x10 view camera in the field and spends considerable time in the darkroom developing film and making fine prints. His final creation is an archivally processed, split-toned, silver print.

Visions from Isle Royale: seeing in silence—

Using an 8×10 camera creates some limitations on what I can photograph in the wilderness (such as where I can go with my equipment and how many exposures I can make before needing to reload film holders in a darkroom). At Isle Royale I had a wilderness cabin to live in and a second smaller cabin where I changed a bedroom into a darkroom for unloading and reloading my film holders each day. Thus I was able to work in a remote wilderness location and expose 250 sheets of 8×10 black and white film. Each day I explored by foot or canoe and was able to work intensely in undistracted silence. I never before had the opportunity to work this way in a wilderness setting.

Besides this great wilderness-photography opportunity, I had the privileges of solitude and silence. I was able to focus entirely on work, meaning I was able to focus on seeing. For me, the creative movement in photography is seeing creatively.

Highlights of my stay at Isle Royale included three fantastic nighttime thunder and lightning shows. The weather was quite hot for me and I enjoyed several refreshing swims in the unusually warm Lake Superior. I remember a magical evening canoeing in the dark on a mirror smooth bay, the only sound made by my paddle in the water, the stars reflecting in the black water.

Each day was different. The wind changed in force and direction. The waves changed with the wind. The sky and clouds were different each day. The great lake changed colors constantly. Each day was new and I hoped to see it as new with each rock and tree I filmed.

This extraordinary occasion to commune intimately with a part of the Isle Royale wilderness was an unusually extended creative opportunity. I was able to create a whole new body of work, perhaps my most mature work yet. It was also a time of spiritual retreat, a time of silence and solitude. It was a time of undistracted attention to the natural world and appreciation of the experience that solitude and silence in the wilderness bring. I hope my photographs pay due respect to this extraordinary island wilderness.

Isle Royale #141

photograph

9¹/₂″ × 7¹/₂″

Isle Royale #39

photograph

7¹/₂″ × 9¹/₂″

Isle Royale #13
photograph
4³/₄″ × 9¹/₂″

Jan Zita Grover

ABOUT THE ARTIST

Jan Zita Grover was born and educated in Northern California. She has lived in Minnesota since 1991. "Like so many other residents of economically depressed northeastern Minnesota," she says, "I piece together my living from a variety of part-time, self-generated jobs: petsitting, book editing, and freelance writing." Her first book, **North Enough: AIDS and Other Clear-cuts** *(Graywolf Press, 1997), won the 1998 Minnesota Book Award for creative nonfiction. Her second book,* **Northern Waters** *(Graywolf Press), was published in fall 1999. She is currently at work on* **Ditched and Drained: A Minnesota Story** *and* **Amity Creek,** *a cultural and natural history of one small watershed in Duluth, Minnesota, where she lives with her six dogs. When she is not at work for pay, she explores the back-country of Pine and Carlton counties.*

138

For weeks afterward, I fell asleep to breakers crashing in the cove below, to the faint human sounds of tour boats slipping across the mouth of Tobin Harbor. I had dreaded re-entry, and I had been right to dread it: traffic proved to be the assault it is, an assault we've accommodated our treacherously adaptable selves to; city sounds, even in my quiet town, rocketed through my skull like grenades. I moved from front bedroom to back, the better to hear those island sounds when I sought sleep. I can hear them still, almost a year later, near dawn, when Duluth has quieted.

I was interested in the interpenetration of human and other animal worlds before going to Isle Royale, but perhaps no place else has been so clearly *the others' world*, one we two leggeds merely visit and then leave to those who dwell there. I liked visiting their world, artfully managed as it is near the largest human habitations. I liked the discomfort it engendered in me, in other people whom I met, so many of our toys and tools withheld. *Here*, the island's deeper inhabitants said, *This is what we give you: TIME.*

That's all: for giving up the human baubles, we're given time.

I like to think I saw the lichens grow. My stay was one with little rain, but each small cup fattened around its raindrop. Watching lichens grow is not a mainland activity. Perhaps it should be. How can a human, with her short lifetime, write meaningfully about a world that unfolds over centuries instead of mere tens of years? How can humans dare to *manage* nature with such evident confidence? We are like children playing at tea party: someone else, after all, will sweep up the remains.

Ephoron Leukon

When I entered the river that mild September evening, the pale creatures, known to anglers as white mayflies, were still streaking toward the surface in the eddies along the riverbank, their bodies angling upward like rocket tracers against the dark water. Once at the surface, they trailed their shucks behind them as they dried their wings, riding the current like spinnakered boats. Then they took to the air, two-tailed males, three-tailed females, joining in midflight, sometimes falling back toward the water as one, then fluttering skyward again, mounting in a near-solid bank four to five feet in height and extending as far up- and downstream as I could see.

The sky was alive with them. They entered my ears, the neck of my shirt. I felt them flutter up the loose legs of my shorts and bat around in my crotch. They crowded behind my glasses and shot up my nostrils. Despite the mosquitoes, who were also out by the millions, seeking their motes of blood, I unbuttoned my shirt and opened the neck wide to funnel mayflies toward to me: I wanted to feel them flutter against my breasts, my throat, my sternum, their touch delicate as single hairs.

By the time I stopped an hour later for water and looked down my shirt front, shoals of dead and dying mayflies had pooled at my waist, wings still beating feebly, their translucent bodies fitted together like stacked spoons.

Artists' Contact Information

James Armstrong
home:
258 East 9th St., Winona, MN 55987
507-454-1759
work:
English Dept., Winona State University, Winona MN
    55987
e-mail:
jarmstrong@vaxz.winona.msus.edu

Amy E. Arntson
home:
N6475 Shorewood Hills Rd., Lake Mills WI 53551
920-648-5255
work:
Art Dept. University of Wisconsin-Whitewater
262-472-1324
e-mail:
arntsona@uwwvax.uww.edu

Julia M. Barello
home:
1845 N. Alameda Blvd., Las Cruces NM 88005
work:
Dept. of Art, NMSU, Williams Hall, Rm 100,
    Las Cruces NM 88003
505-646-1705
e-mail:
jbarello@nmsu.edu

Marilyn Mallory Brandenburger
home/work:
2221 Desmond Dr, Decatur GA 30033
404-325-4302
e-mail:
mmbrand@prodigy.net

Alain Briot
home:
PO Box 520, Chinle AZ 86503
520-674-5276
work:
800-949-7983
e-mail:
abstudio@cybertrails.com
website:
www.cybertrails/~abstudio

Diane Canfield Bywaters
home:
1908 Main St.
Stevens Point, WI 54481
715-344-1713
work:
Dept. of Art & Design, Univ. of Wisconsin-Stevens
    Point, Stevens Point WI 55481
e-mail:
dbywater@uwsp.edu
website:
www.Bywaters.com

Judith Corning
work:
960 Ventura Ave, Albany CA 94707-2542
510-526-6367
e-mail:
GeneJudy@aol.com

Joe M. Cronan
work:
2245 Nimblewill Church Rd., Dahlonega GA 30533

Lee Dassler
home:
12 Big Hill Rd., Otisfield, ME 04270
207-743-7620
work:
The McLaughlin Garden, PO Box 16, South Paris
    ME 04281
207-743-8820
e-mail:
mclgardn@megalink.net

Deborah Eddy
home/work:
PO Box 363, Soquel CA 95073
831-476-8341
e-mail:
eddyart@earthlink.net

Sylvia "Tykie" Ganz
home/work:
10290 Seagrape Way, Palm Beach Garden FL 33418
561-622-5617

Jan Zita Grover
home/work:
109 S. 18th Ave. East, Duluth, MN 55801
218-728-9723
e-mail:
jzgrover@cpinternet.com
fax:
218-728-9732

Ladislav R. Hanka
home/work:
1005 Oakland Dr., Kalamazoo MI 49008
616-388-5631

Elizabeth Holster
home:
727 East A St., Iron Mt. MI 49801
906-779-2592
e-mail:
bholster@hotmail.com

Louis Jenkins
home:
101 Clover St., Duluth MN 55812
218-724-6382
e-mail:
louis@skypoint.com

Gendron Jensen
home:
PO Box 194, Vadito NM 87579-0194
505-587-1041
work:
505-587-1046

Gerald J. Korte
home:
1577 52nd St. SE, Saint Cloud, MN 56304
320-252-6086
e-mail:
gkorte@stcloudstate.edu

Jeff Korte
home:
5229 Shoreview Ave., Minneapolis MN 55417
612-724-7947
e-mail:
ljkorte@earthlink.net.

Joyce Koskenmaki
home:
1100 Hill St., Hancock MI 49930
906-483-3183
work:
Suomi College, Hancock MI 49930
906-487-7375

Sheila Larkin
home:
PO Box 502, Oconomowoc, WI 53066
262-569-5154
e-mail:
SheLarkin@aol.com

Gary Lawless
home:
617 East Neck Rd. Nobleboro ME 04555
207-563-8531
work:
Gulf of Maine Books, 134 Maine St., Brunswick ME
  04011
207-729-5083
e-mail:
chimfarm@gwi.net

Greg McHuron
home/work:
350 E. Cottonwood Dr., Jackson WY 83001-9201
307-733-6210
website:
www.newsom.com/McHuron

Melanie Parke
home/work:
The Chief Studio, 7325 Chief Rd., Kaleva MI 49645
231-889-6134

George Provost
home:
PO Box 230821, Anchorage AK 99523-0821
907-349-6743
e-mail:
George@Provost.com

Wayne Rice
home:
PO Box 746, Dolores CO 81323
970-564-9698
e-mail:
desarts@fone.net

Robert Root
work:
Dept. of English, Central Michigan University,
    Mt. Pleasant MI 48859
517-774-3103
e-mail:
Robert.L.Root@cmich.edu
website:
www.chsbs.cmich.edu/Eng/BRoot
fax:
517-774-1271

Richard Schilling
home/work:
3112 Allison Dr., Loveland CO 80538
970-667-5945
e-mail:
Rschil8433@aol.com

Eddie Soloway
home/work:
PO Box G745, Santa Fe, NM 87502
505-466-6030
e-mail:
soloway@anaturaleye.com
website:
www.anaturaleye.com

Rick Stevens
home/work:
171 Orchard Dr., Sparta MI 49345
616-887-0251
e-mail:
rlacuart@aol.com

Keith Taylor
home:
1715 Dexter Ave., Ann Arbor MI 48103
734-665-5341

Dan Urbanski
home/work:
250 Hubbell, Silver City MI 49953
906-885-5895
e-mail:
dfurbski@up.net
website:
www.ontonagon.com/mi/silverimage/welcome.html

Gijsbert van Frankenhuyzen
home/work:
7409 Clark, Bath MI 48808
517-641-6690
e-mail:
robbyn@voyager.net
website:
my.voyager.net/robbyn

Jennifer Williams
home:
314A S. 3rd St., LaCrosse WI 54601
608-796-0342
work:
Art Dept. University of Wisconsin-LaCrosse, LaCrosse
    WI 54601
608-785-8236
e-mail:
williams.jenn@uwlax.edu

Wanda Zuchowski-Schick
129 Eagle Point Rd., Rossford OH 43460
419-666-5820
e-mail:
wshick129@aol.com

I've been here just two weeks and I've seen Lake Superior as calm as glass and as rough and fierce as an open sea, then completely engulfed in fog. I've enjoyed each and lived every day to the fullest. It has been my dream come true. To exist uninterrupted in this peaceful wilderness setting, makes my heart sing.

Isle Royale, I've never known a place like you. Your ancient trees and lush undergrowth, your ever changing sea, the white throated sparrow with its familiar song. The moose, in velvet, that paid me no never mind. The little fox that came to the door and gazed into my eyes. And the wonderful loons I heard so often at evening time. All these, unforgettable.

this is my last day, going with the traditions of these journal entries. There is much to say, much to tell, but most of it has been done in the pages before mine. It has been a brief, two week love-affair, a romance of blinding passion, with this place, this rock and land, and sun light. Being here has been like painting naked, leaving all the barriers behind, allowing all the elemen to touch and mark us, to mark me. I worked on small masonite panels, hiked a camped on Lookout Louise for two nights, an watched the full moon rise over Rock Ha a flame of cadmium in a lavender sky, with warm currents carrying summer scents through my tent. It was awaken to be alone, to have reverence for the moose and her calf that often was in m path, to be silent and humble. The residency is a unique time for gifting ours these things. A responsibility comes wi it, the residency, but often in our rout or in our constant maneuvering arou obstacles to do our life's calling, we neg the important parts of our processes to allow ourselves to fail, to make mista to screw up. And also, to not produce the residency is wonderful for these things read these writings my first awe- struck night in the cabin, and was a instant comfort as an invisible group o comrades, companions telling their t